MAP OF NANTUCKET

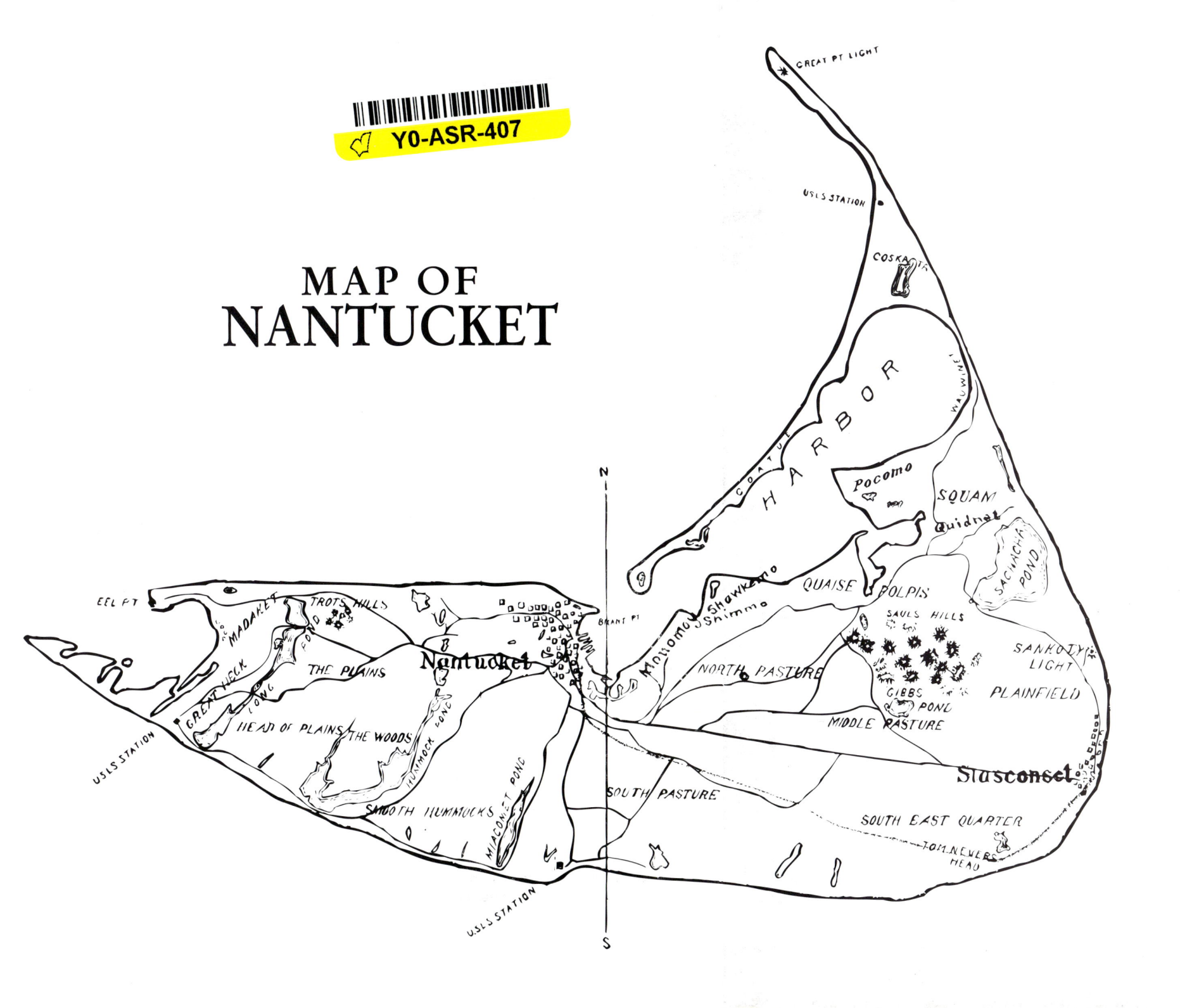

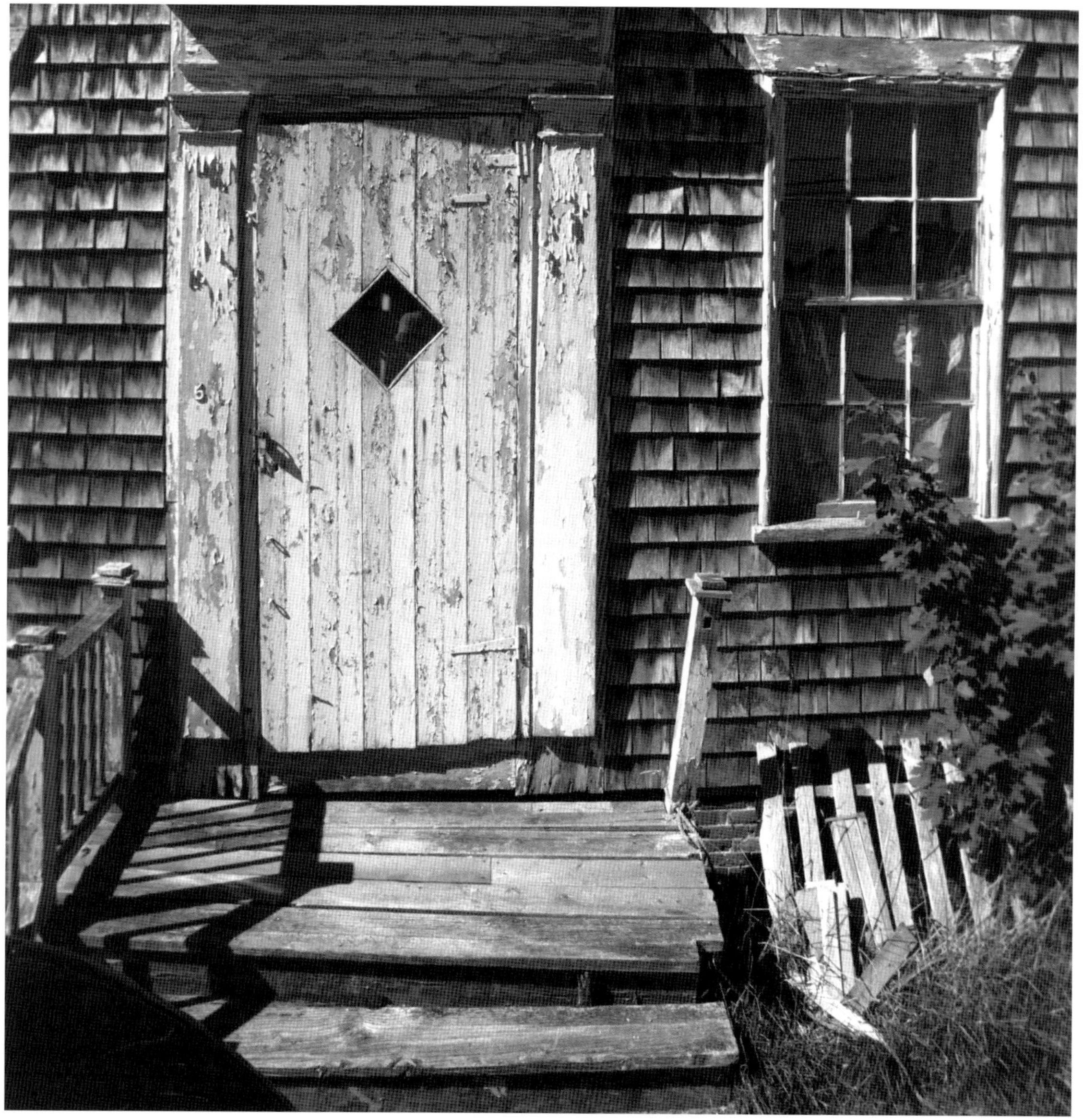

VANISHING

PASSING COMPLETELY FROM EXISTENCE

PASSING QUICKLY FROM SIGHT

CAUSING TO DISAPPEAR

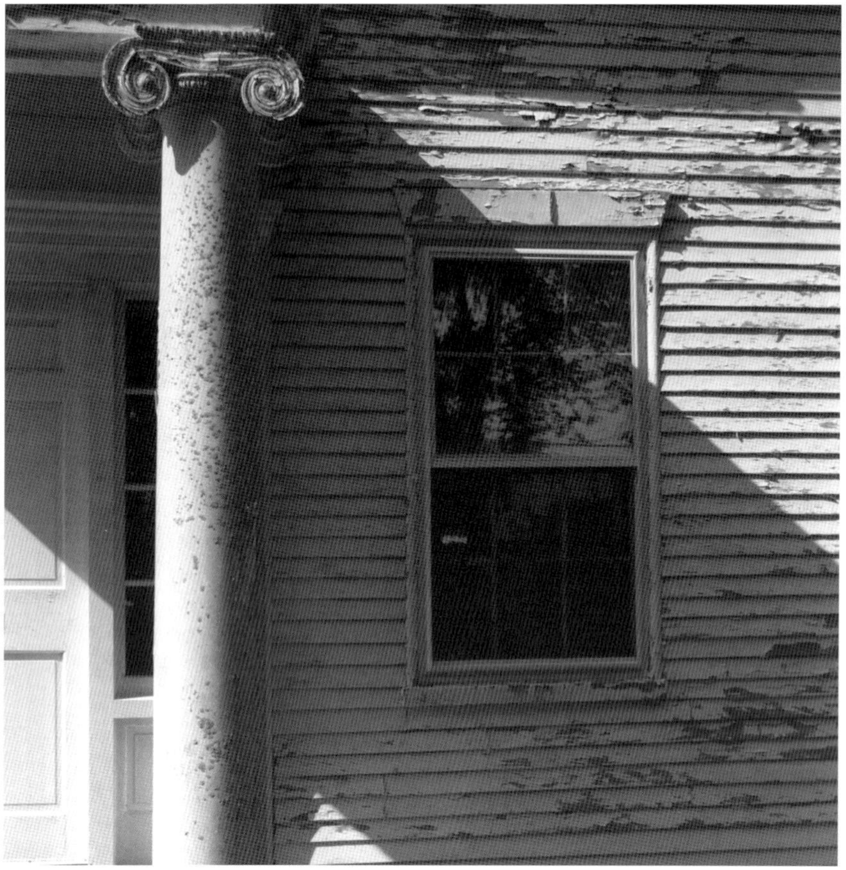

NANTUCKET VANISHING

PHOTOGRAPHS JIM DUNLAP

INTRODUCTION CARY HAZLEGROVE

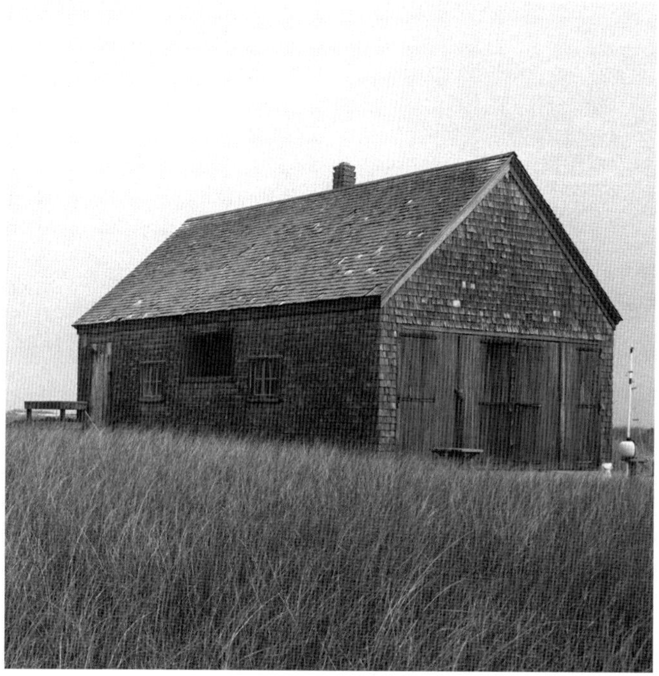

CONTENTS

PREFACE

INTRODUCTION

FOREWORD

PHOTOGRAPHS

EPILOGUE

INDEX

ACKNOWLEDGMENTS

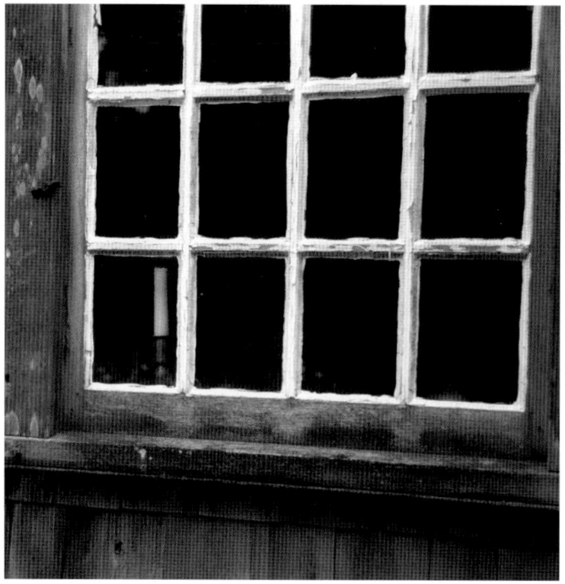

PREFACE

"She sells sea shells by the sea shore."

Nantucket always sells me her seaside beauty, sweeping me in with her arms of salty air, willow harps, rolling moors, and shining shingles. For forty years I have enjoyed the warmth of summer sand and the bleakness of winter days. Her fog bathes me in security and her northeasters keep me dancing.

Over the years I have photographed her many faces, not with serious interest but with a desire to satisfy my love of the island. Time made itself available so I set myself on a more serious journey. I have tried to capture not the people of the island but rather what they have built and what Mother nature brought forth for us to see. Houses, shacks, and sheds have been built with every shingle and nail coming from across the ocean to join the rugosa roses, blue stem grasses and bear berry carpeting.

What I cherish most is the precarious balance established between conservation of open spaces and development for mankind. The island's finite resources are tested every day, but I am optimistic that future generations can enjoy what I have, if greed and ego are held at bay.

So why do these structures appear here? They are not majestic or grand. They do not represent those sights familiar to many. Many are photographs of the underdogs, ignored by the human hand or beaten by the forces of nature over years of use and neglect. Some built for people, some built for forgotten uses, they are becoming vestiges of the past. Let us cherish and preserve what we have. Let us save both the vistas and the structures built before us.

Jim Dunlap

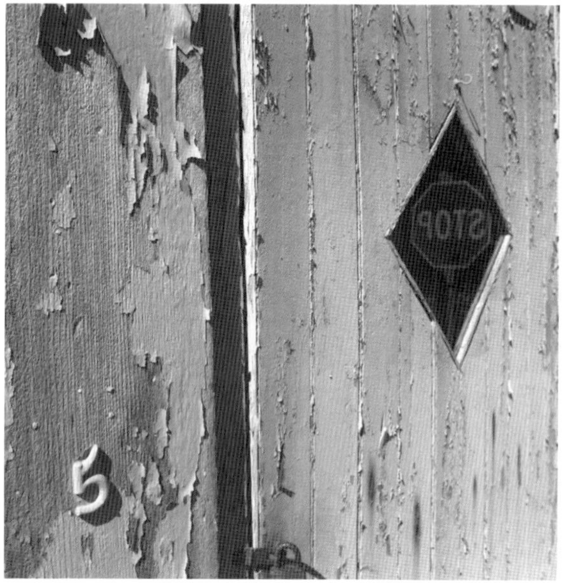
STOP
5

INTRODUCTION

How do you explain a compulsion to photograph peeling paint and decaying structures? That you are truly inspired by dilapidation? Is it that we live in such a pristine, manicured environment that we need these visuals to stimulate our connection to the past? In what most people would consider a run down eyesore, Jim Dunlap has found poetry. He has combed the islands of Nantucket, Muskeget and Tuckernuck, collecting images that reveal to us a piece of our past.

In the attempt to preserve our historically significant heritage with strict guidelines in design and "building with Nantucket in mind," the island is awash in homogeneity.

We are surrounded by newly built, large, and out-of-scale structures that stand empty for eight months of the year. Jim Dunlap's photographs offer a refreshing and nostalgic glimpse of the "old" Nantucket--Nantucket "then," with structures that were harmoniously conceived to withstand the harsh environment that Nantucket dishes out. It's hard to believe that these are contemporary photographs.

We are fortunate to have Jim's thoughtful eye. He has captured a longing--a longing for open spaces, an easier life, a simpler time. Cherish these feelings.

Cary Hazlegrove

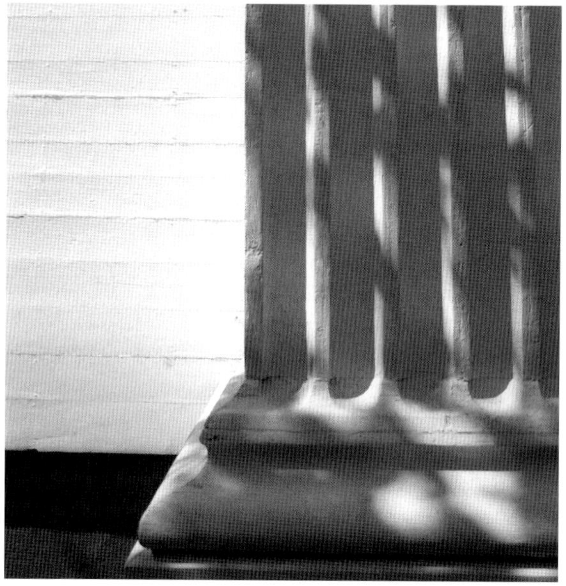

FOREWORD

Nantucket, when seen for the first time, engenders awe. The glorious homes and the seaside shanties. The original cobblestones. The commercial buildings intact after a devastating fire over 150 years ago. The island's uniqueness elevates her to a national treasure different from Williamsburg, Jamestown, or Sturbridge, each of which is unique, but not original. Nantucket is a truly original gem, and for that, priceless in the eyes of the beholder. For the viewer of these photographs, an explanation of that reality draws us back through her history.

Nantucket was born during the last ice age some 30,000 years ago. She rests roughly 30 miles off the continental United States, a humble pile of sand and glacial debris comprising some 30,000 acres. Portugal, her nearest European neighbor, lies 3000 miles to the east. To the south, the Greater Antilles fall 1500 miles below her southern shore.

Nantucket's commercial origins illustrate friendly relations between the settlers (as we think of them) and the natives. Ten original proprietors from England bought the western end of the island from Thomas Mayhew of Martha's Vineyard in 1659. Once on shore, they found the indigenous Indians willing to sell more of the island, enabling the initial settlers to arrive during the autumn of that year. Tristram Coffin, Sr., one of the original proprietors, determined that the island would be suitable for permanent habitation. To some degree these families wanted freedom from the Puritan domination in Massachusetts and independence to raise their children as they saw fit. It is remarkable that these men, mostly farmers and tradesmen, settled to work the poorest soils in New England. More astounding yet is that they knew nothing of the sea that surrounded them on all sides.

For a number of years, the settlers let newcomers buy property on the island only if they came armed with the trades and skills needed to support the community.

Thus self-sufficiency thrived, and over the long term gave rise to a local culture of independence and individualism that remains evident today. One might speculate that this character results both from the island's isolation and from the ethnic and religious stock (English and predominantly Quaker by 1700) that populated her lands in the early days of European immigration. For the next 130 years these English Quakers became a majority, influencing everything from language to architecture, clothing to mercantile practices, as well as social values that stressed frugality and simplicity.

It was the Indians, initially, who taught white Nantucketers to live off the sea. Their centuries-old skills in fishing and along-shore whaling were adapted and, despite the native peoples' demise by about 1800, made the island one of the richest communities in the United States by 1830. Nantucketers ranked among the world's most skilled sailors, dominating the Pacific waters during the late 1700s and into the early part of the next century. It was the wealth from the sea that gave the Islanders the capacity to create the extraordinary residential and commercial buildings we enjoy today.

Early island architecture reflects both the geographic and religious sensibilities of the earliest white inhabitants. The island's first structures were copies of English styles familiar to the settlers. Four known "English" houses survive today, including the Jethro Coffin house, known as the "Oldest House," at 1 Sunset Hill (built in 1686). Next came the "lean-to's," of which over seventy survive today, including the Richard Gardner III house on West Chester Street, built in 1722 to 24. Over the years, unadorned and simple structures suitable to the Quaker aesthetic evolved into "traditional" or "typical" Nantucket houses, a style that prevailed from the 1760s to the 1830s. More than 170 of these homes exist today. By the 1830s the Quakers and their way of life had faded from the island, leaving their structures as the most tangible evidence of their far-reaching influence.

Penetrated by the outside world and stirred by new-found wealth, the Islanders and their structures soon began to reflect a broader, more liberal interpretation of taste. Colonial, Federal, Gambrel, Greek Revival, and Gothic buildings began to appear, with cupolas, hip roofs, fan doorways and other decidedly non-austere features. Even the Victorian period, with its "gingerbread" flourishes, inspired a small number of structures. More than 800 homes and commercial buildings built before 1900 exist today. We are privileged to delight in the wealth of architectural beauty.

What forces helped preserve this astounding inventory of historic structures? Nature set the island at sea, providing protective isolation and preventing rapid changes in culture and character. As the loss of sail gave way to the advent of modern transportation — from steam ferry, diesel ferry, and gas-turbine ferry to the airplane — much of that isolation tumbled. Today the island is truly isolated only in fog or severe storms. But a more important inhibitor of change was the deep depression Nantucket suffered following the decline of the whaling industry. Other calamities followed: The Great Fire of 1846, which destroyed most of the downtown commercial district; the Civil War, and two World Wars.

Perhaps nothing defined the changed world for Nantucket more than the discovery of oil in Pennsylvania in 1856. Mother nature's bounty was now found from within the earth's crust rather than from her multitudes of seafaring mammals. Whale-oil candles gave way to kerosene lanterns and ultimately the nation became dependent on hydrocarbon fuels for the internal combustion engine. As a sign of tenacity to keep change at bay, the automobile was banned from the island until 1918.

Nantucket's economy finally came out of its slumber in the 1950s. The dismal years prior to the postwar period ultimately provided a measure of poetic justice for the economic suffering the island had seen. A century of economic struggle had provided superb protection for the finest craftsmanship of the age. The structural and architectural integrity of the original buildings, coupled with an economy that did not support rebuilding, underwrote the preservation of the original designs.

In 1955, the State of Massachusetts passed enabling legislation permitting Nantucket to establish the first historic district in the state. Further restrictions came with island wide zoning and architectural control in 1972. Along with this landmark state and local protection, two organizations have played significant roles in maintaining the culture and character of Nantucket. The Nantucket Historical Association (founded in 1894) and the Nantucket Conservation Foundation (founded in 1963) both work diligently to preserve the island's history and conserve her open space. To ensure continued, long-term success in these endeavors, both need considerable financial support from both Islanders and visitors.

This book of photographs is just a small contribution to those noble efforts. I hope to create a different awareness and appreciation of the island.

Jim Dunlap

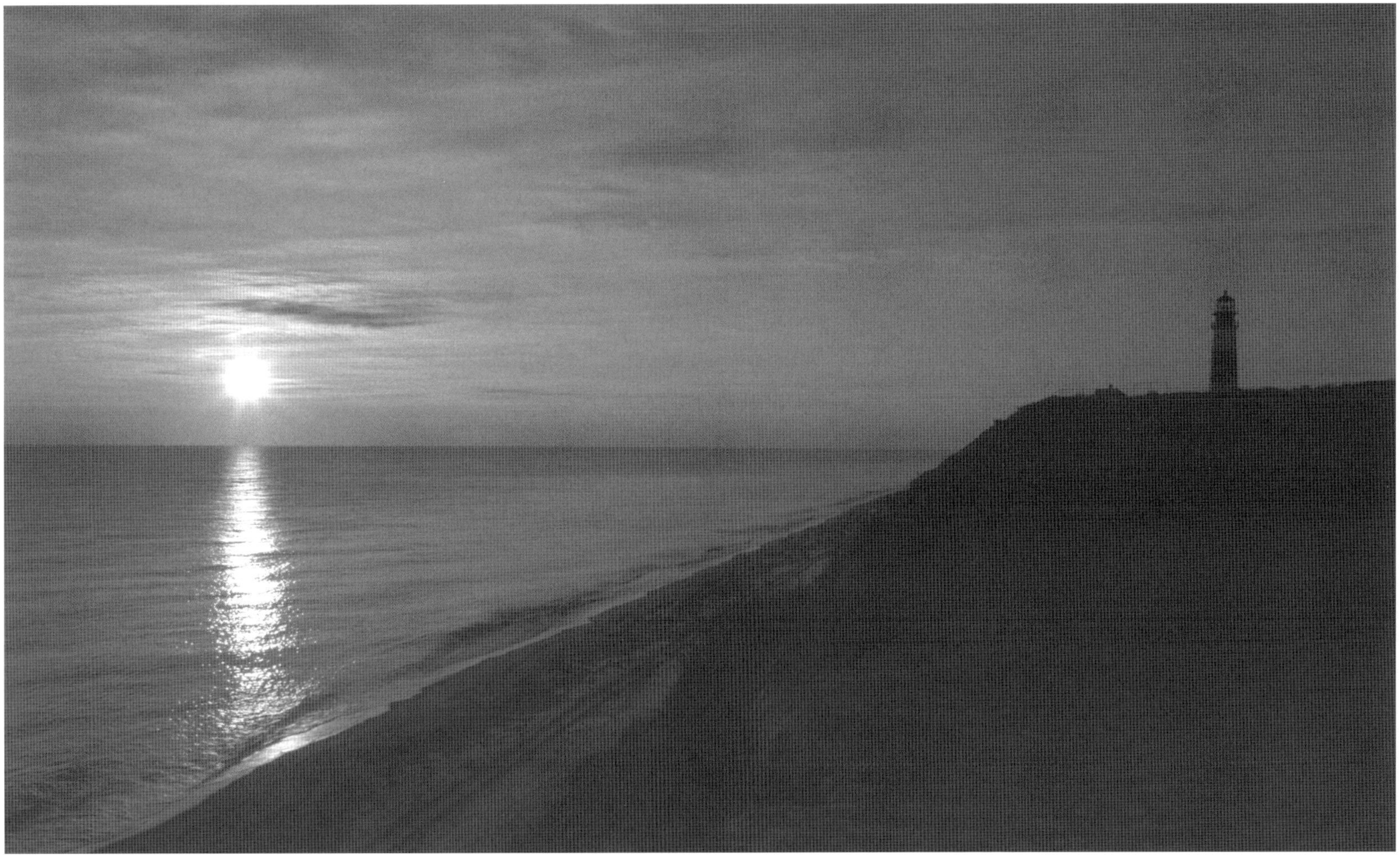

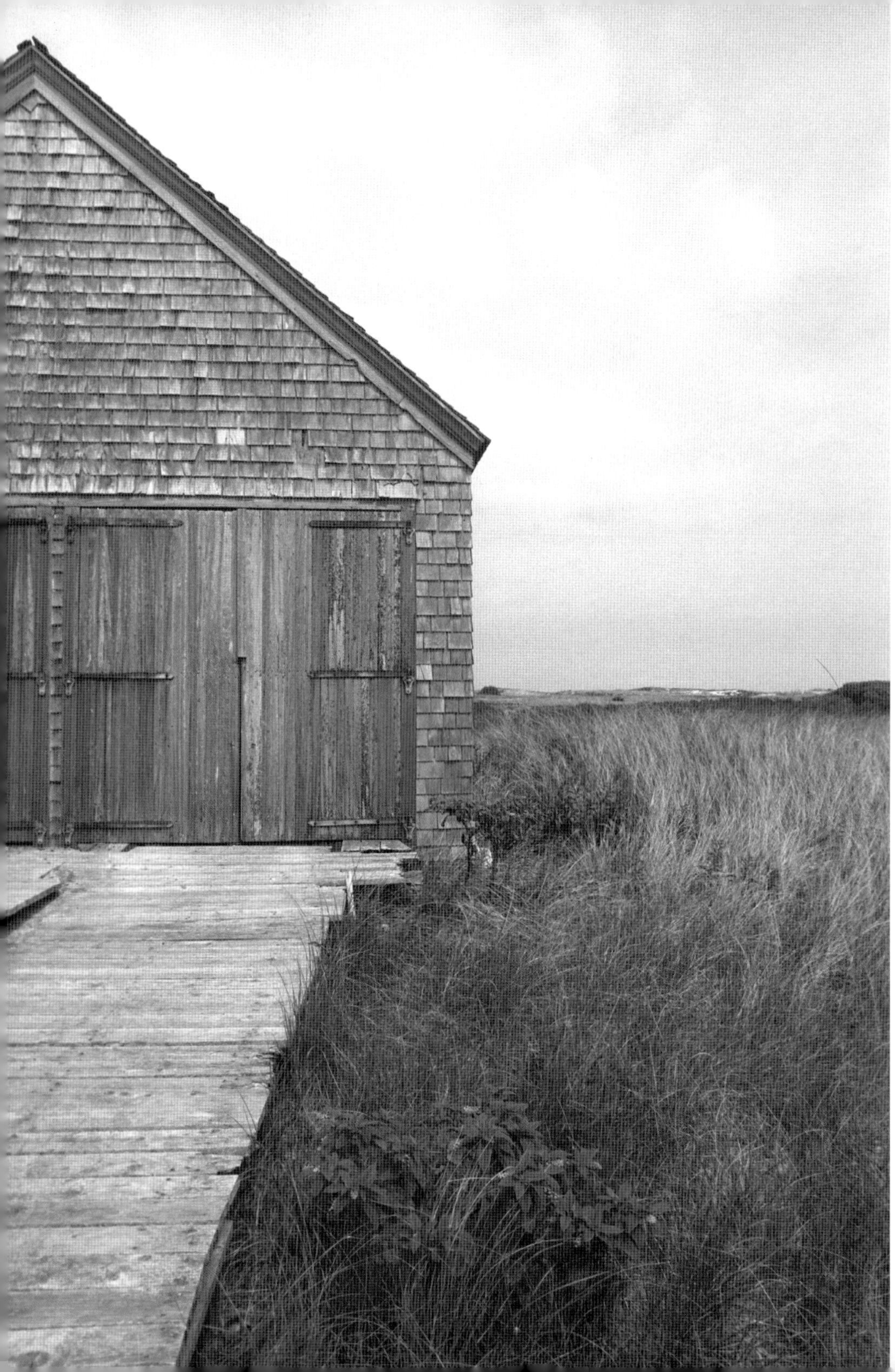

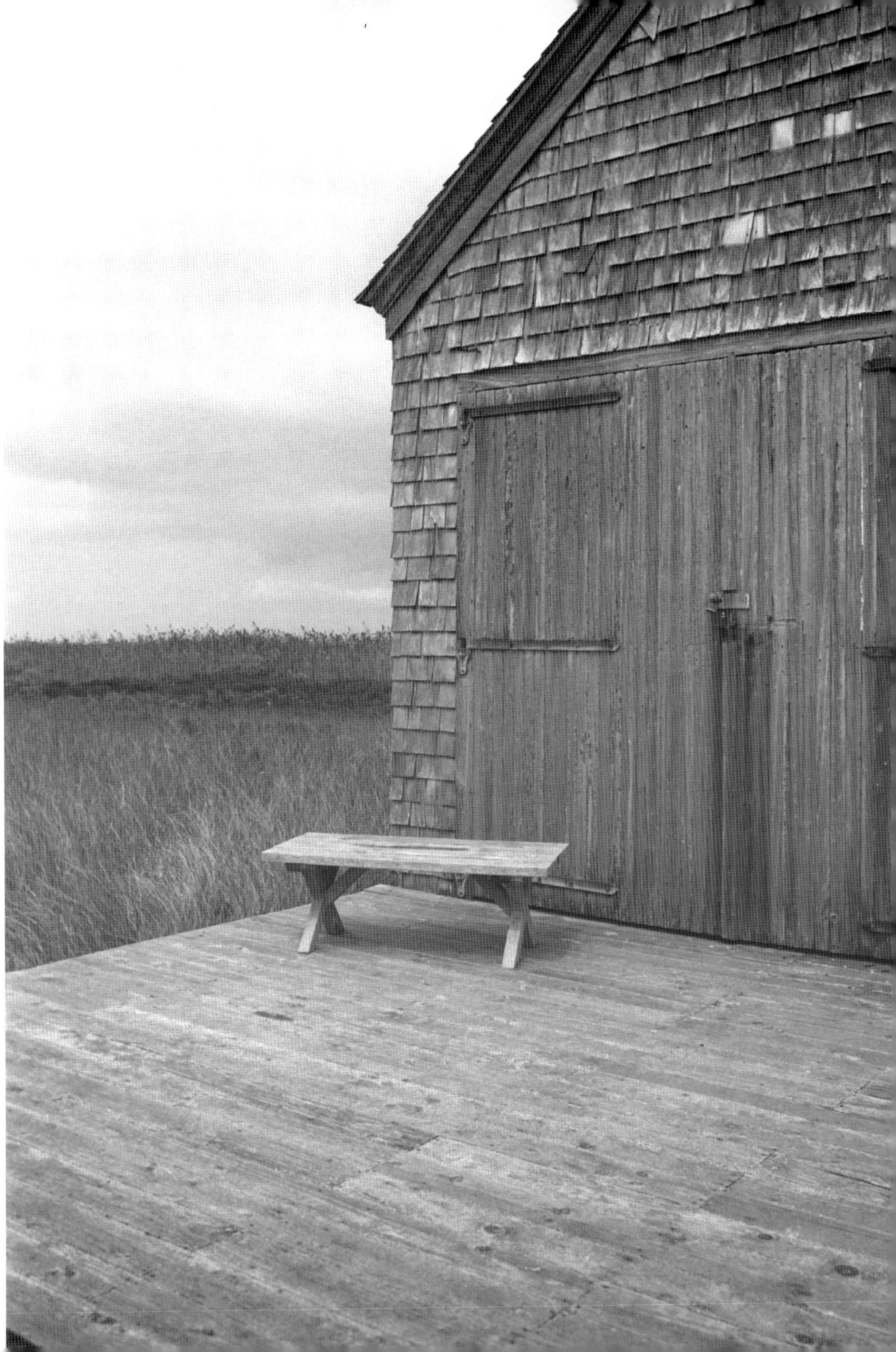

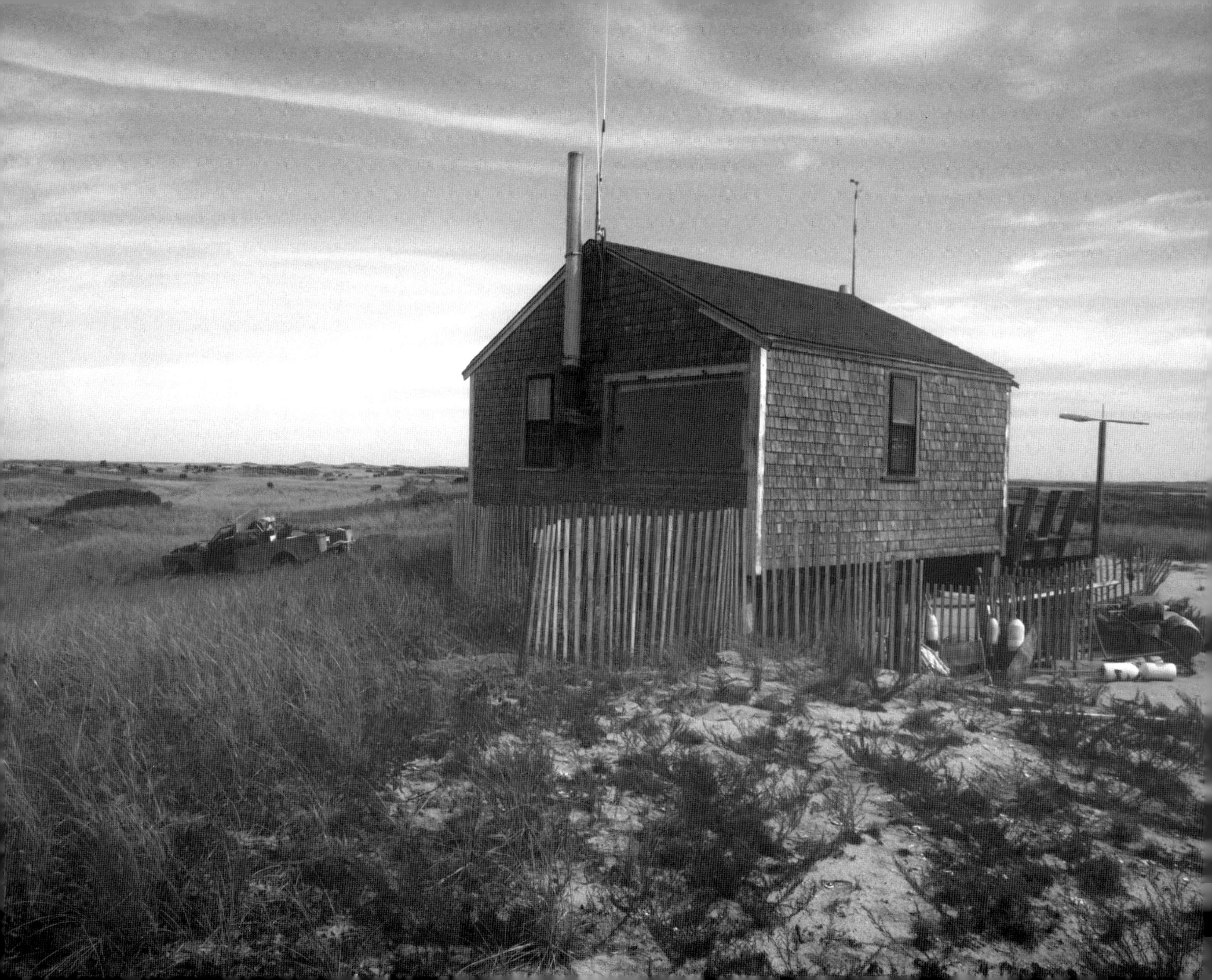

MUSKEGET 41°20.3
           70°18.5

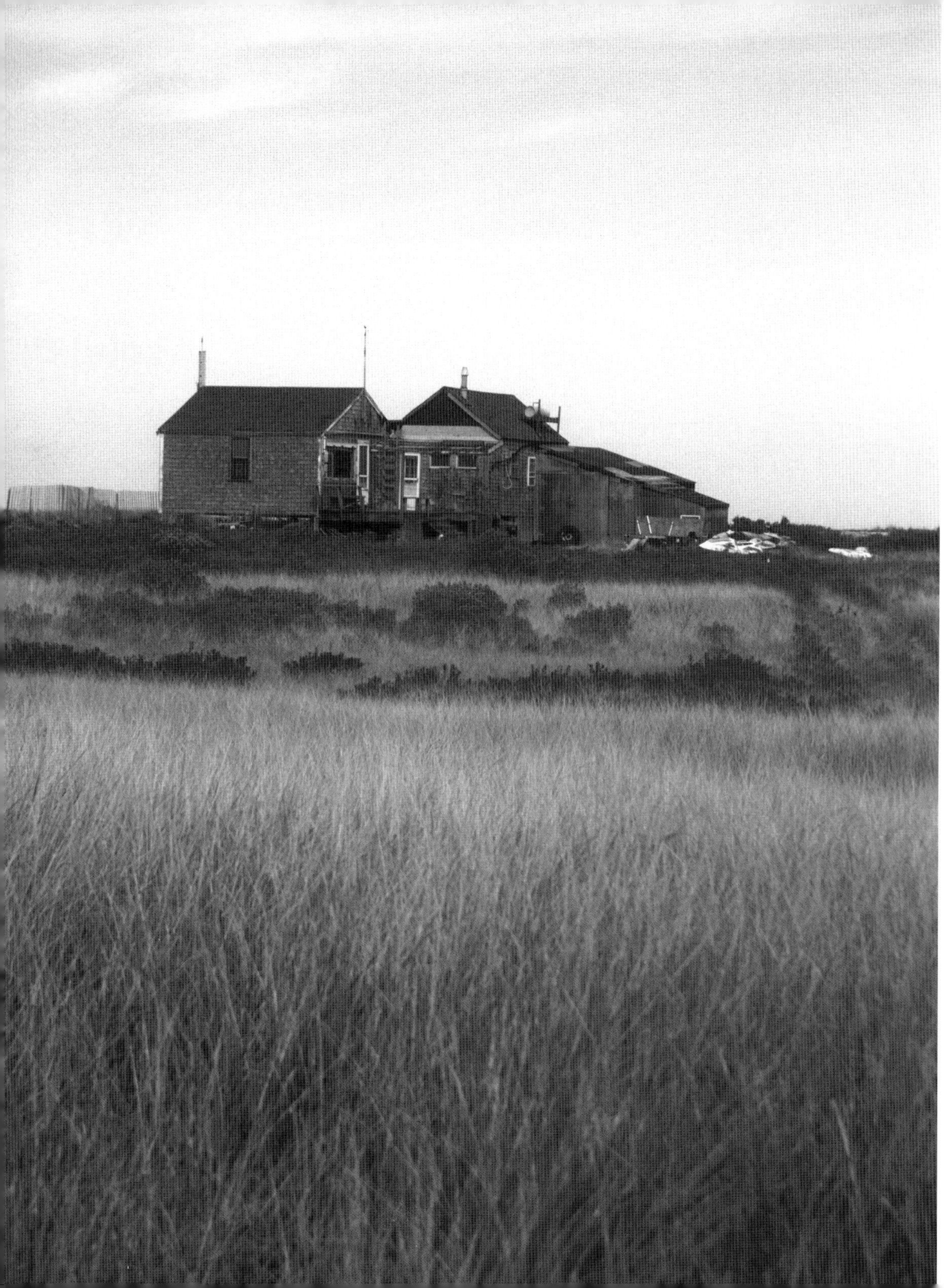

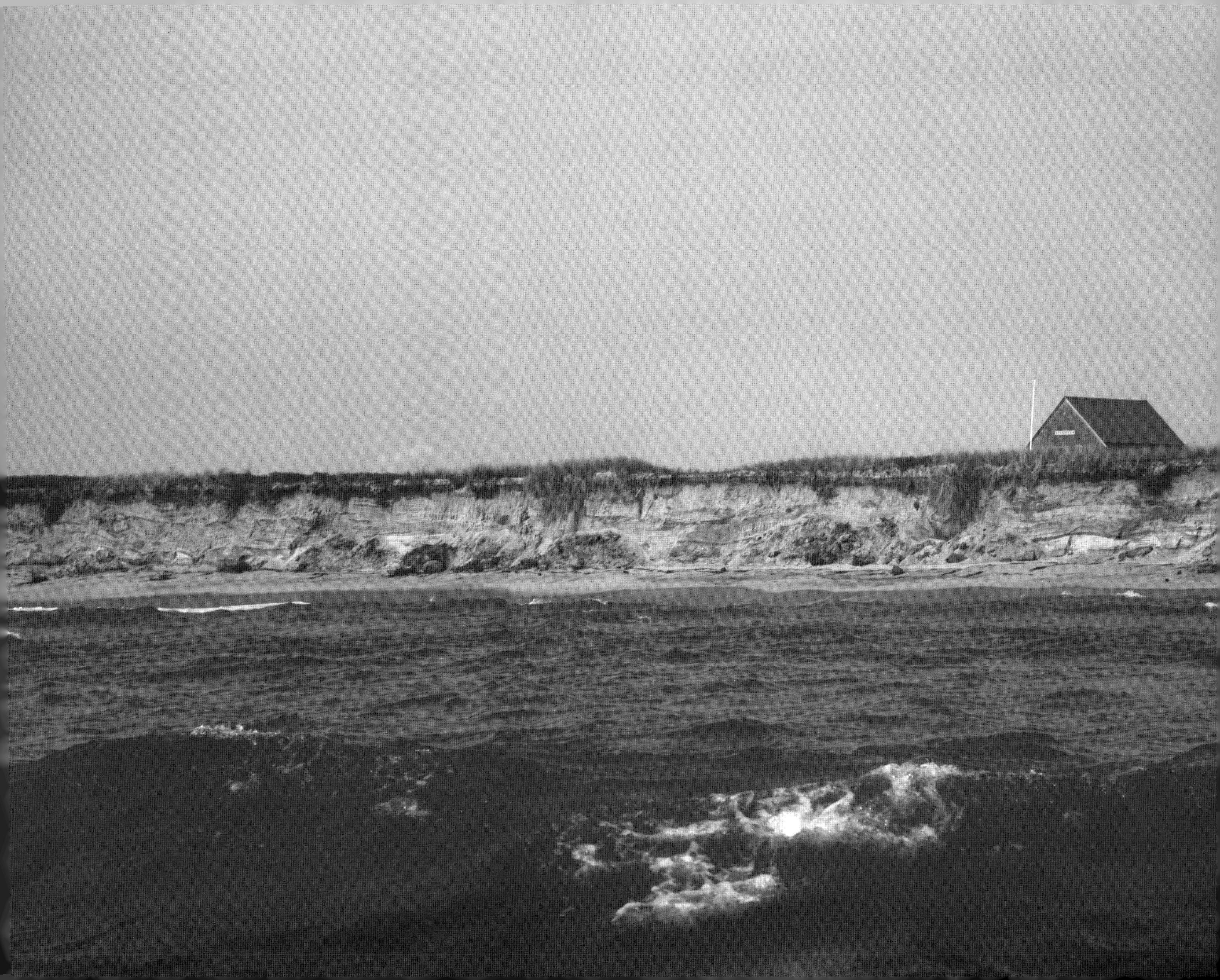

10

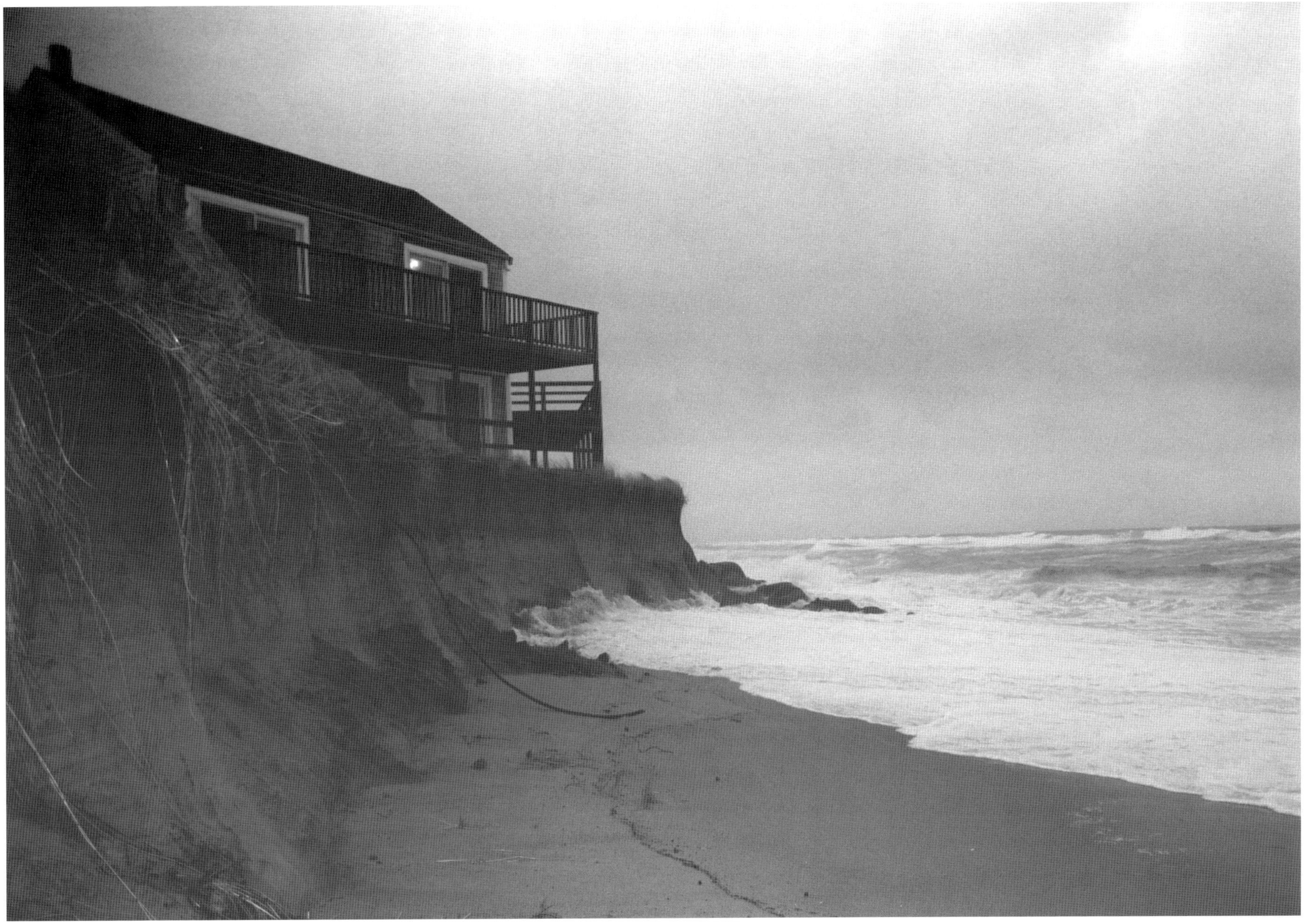

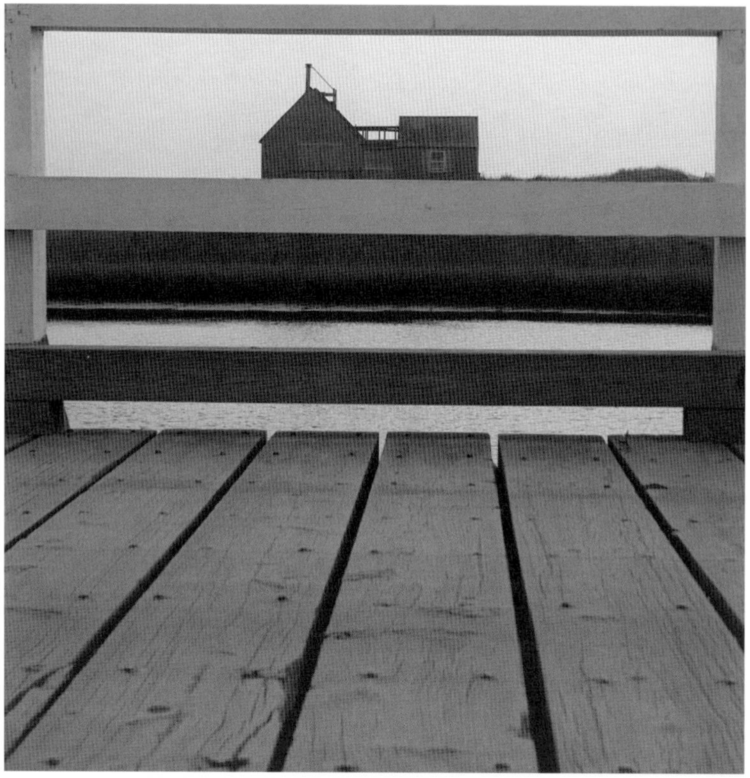

13

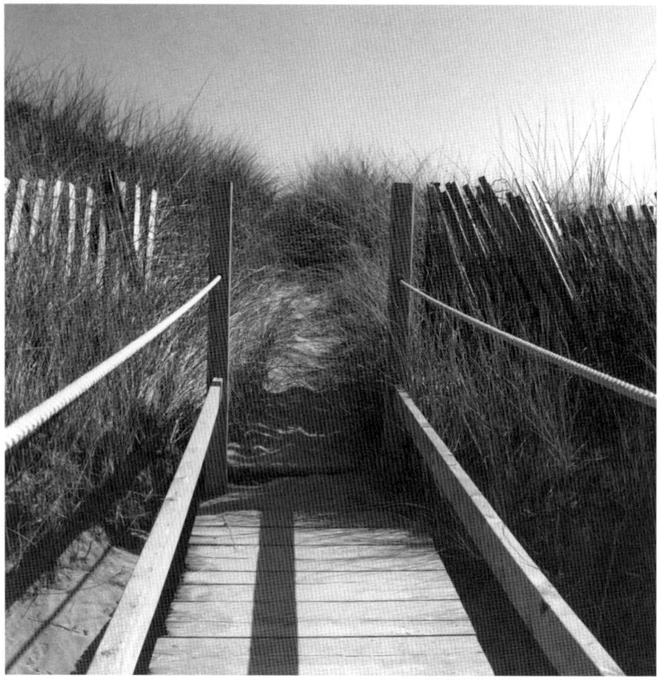

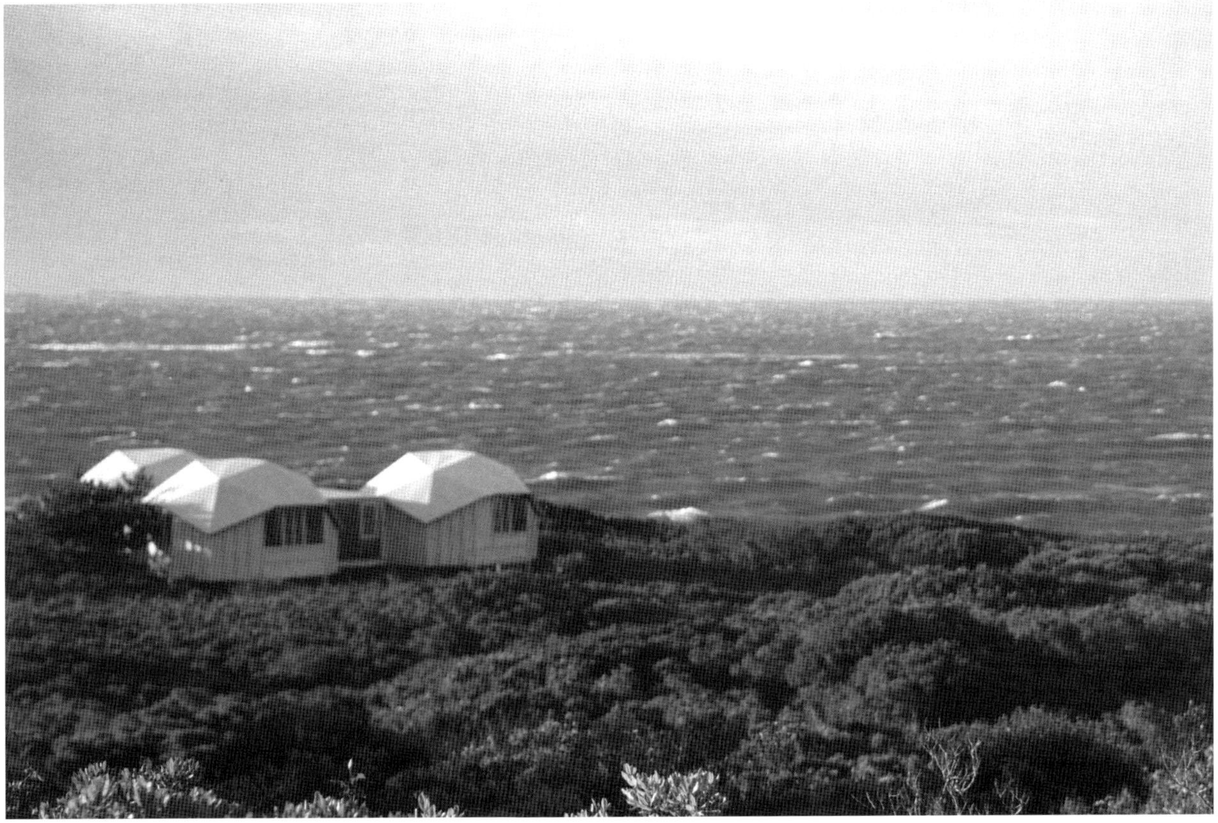

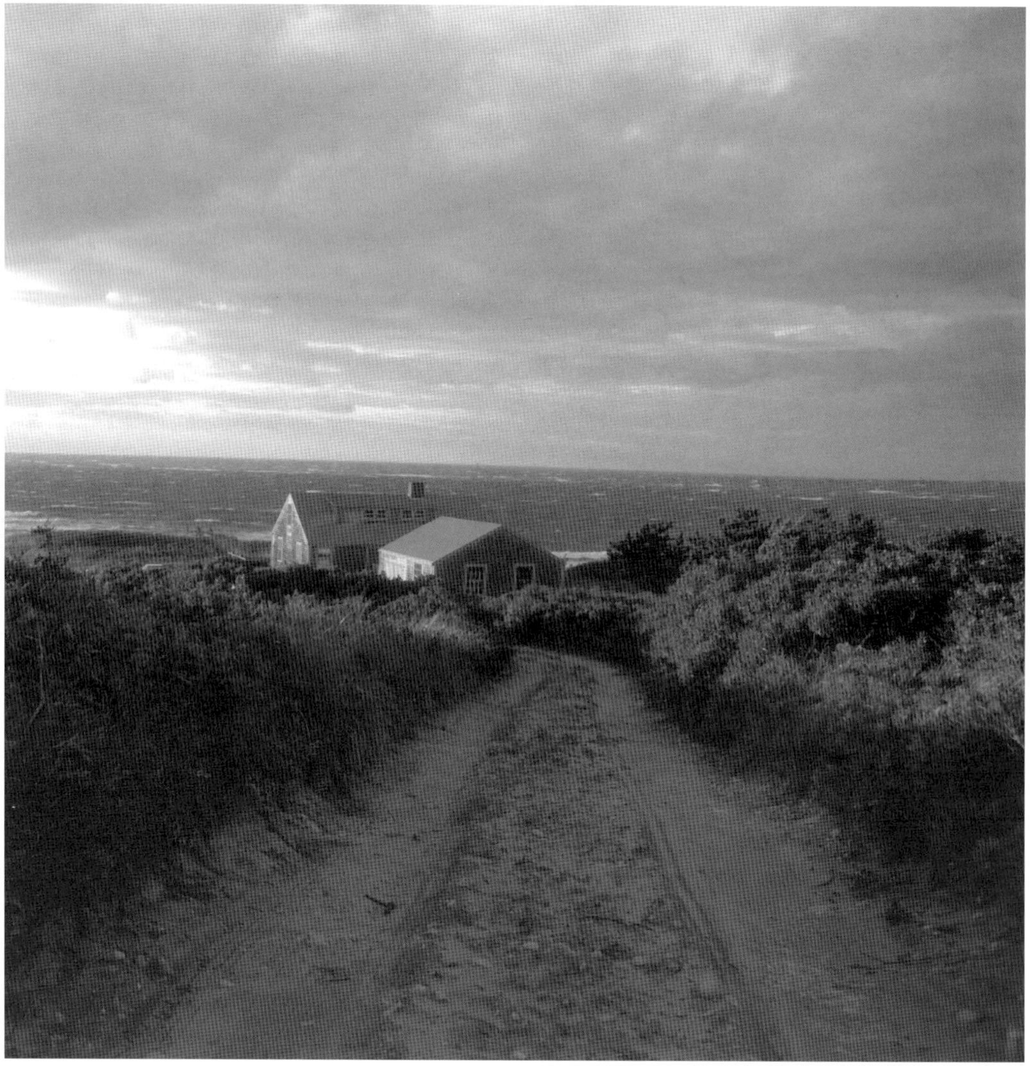

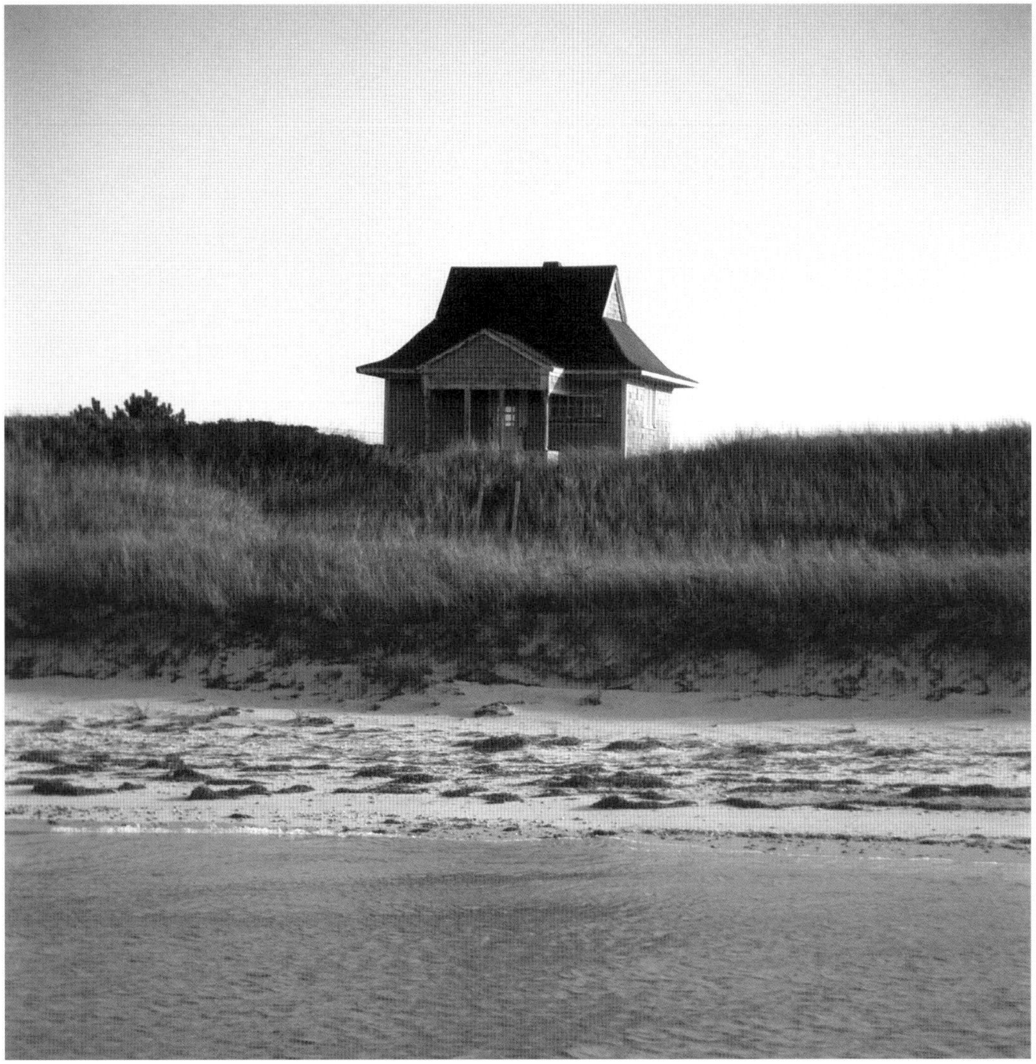

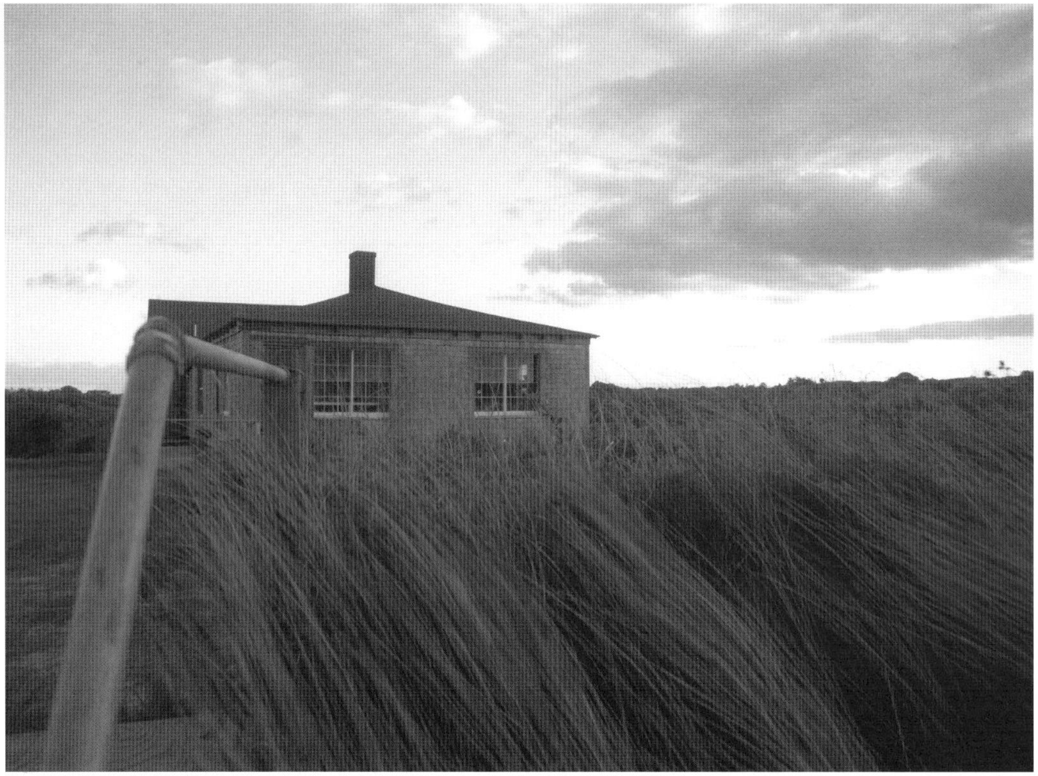

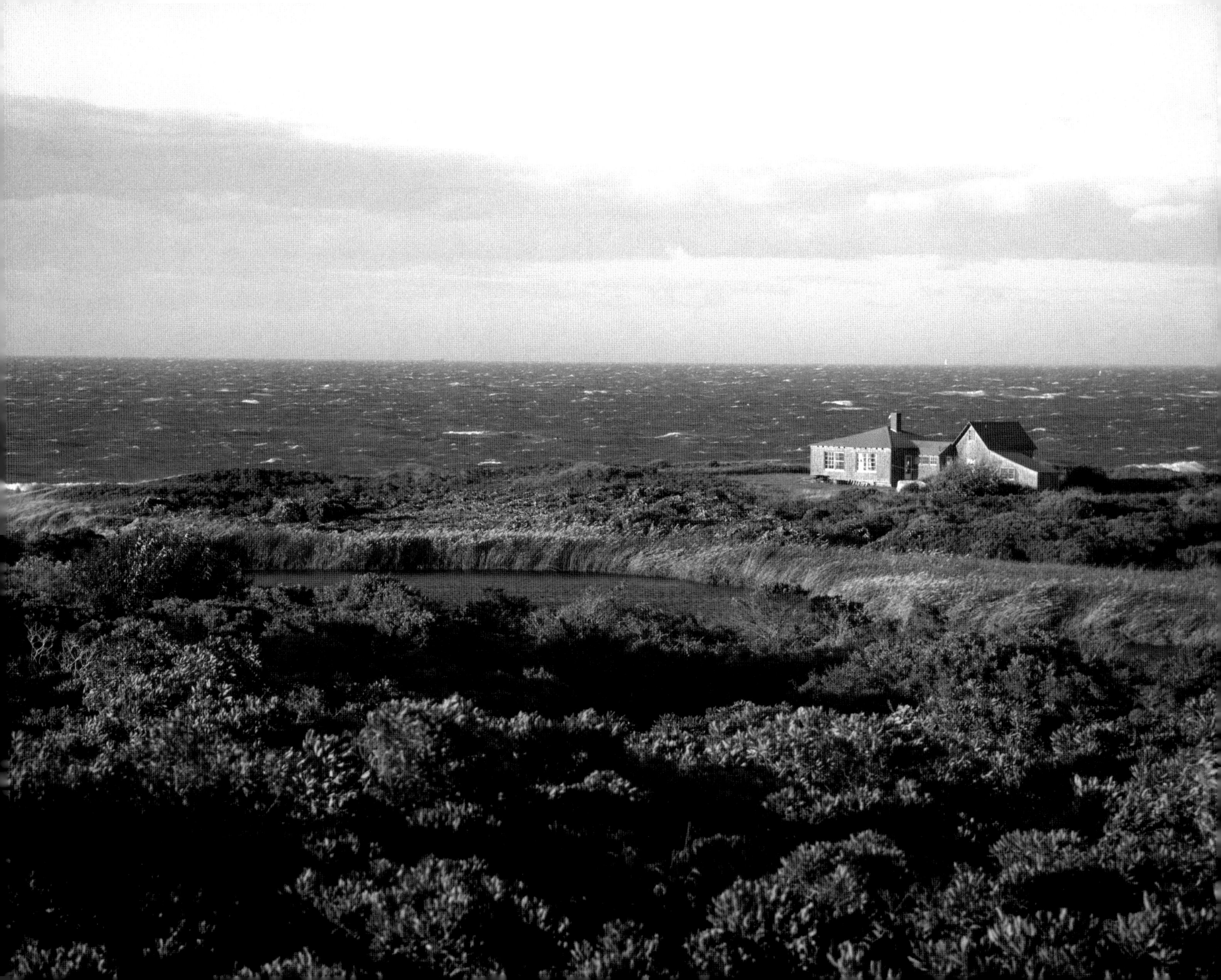

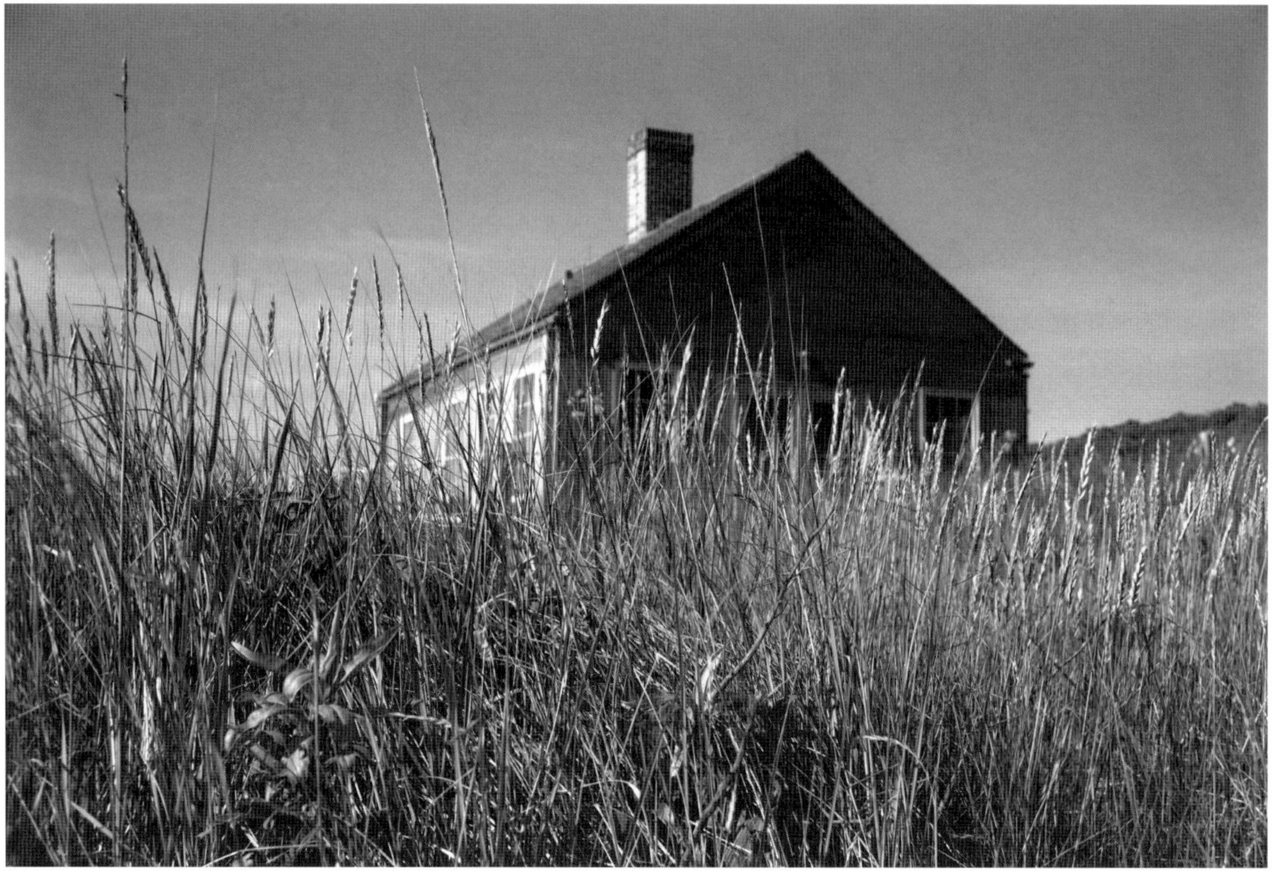

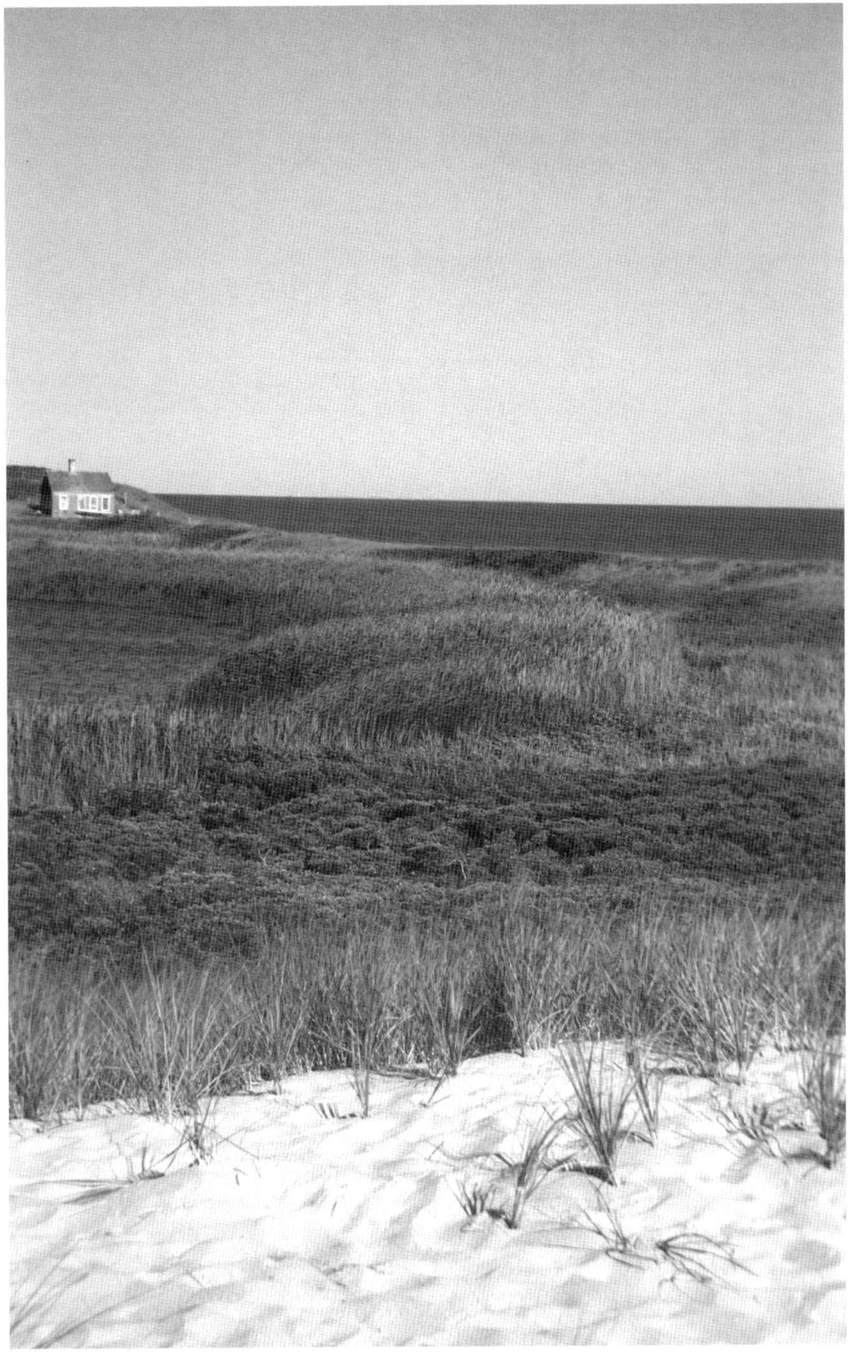

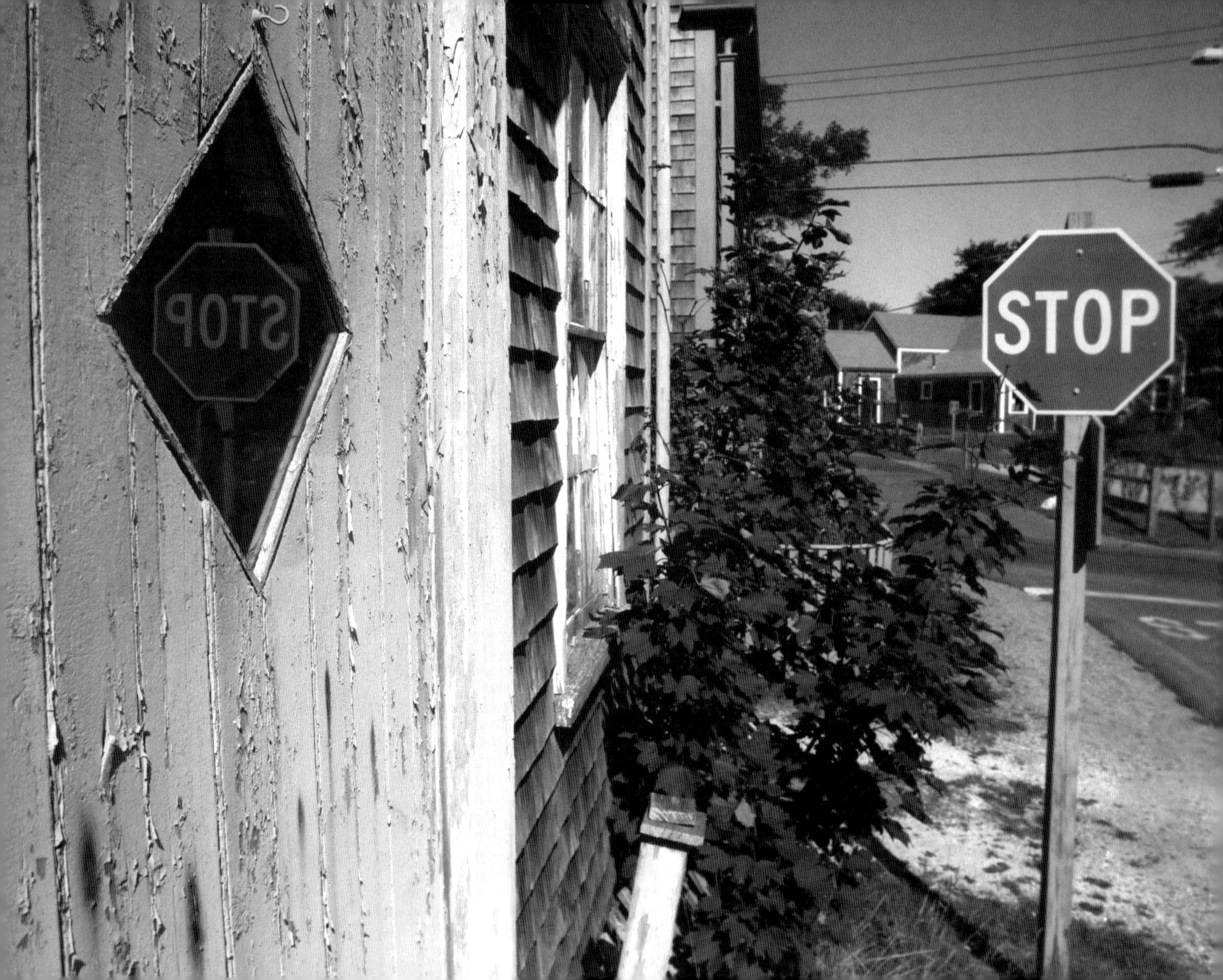
STOP
STOP

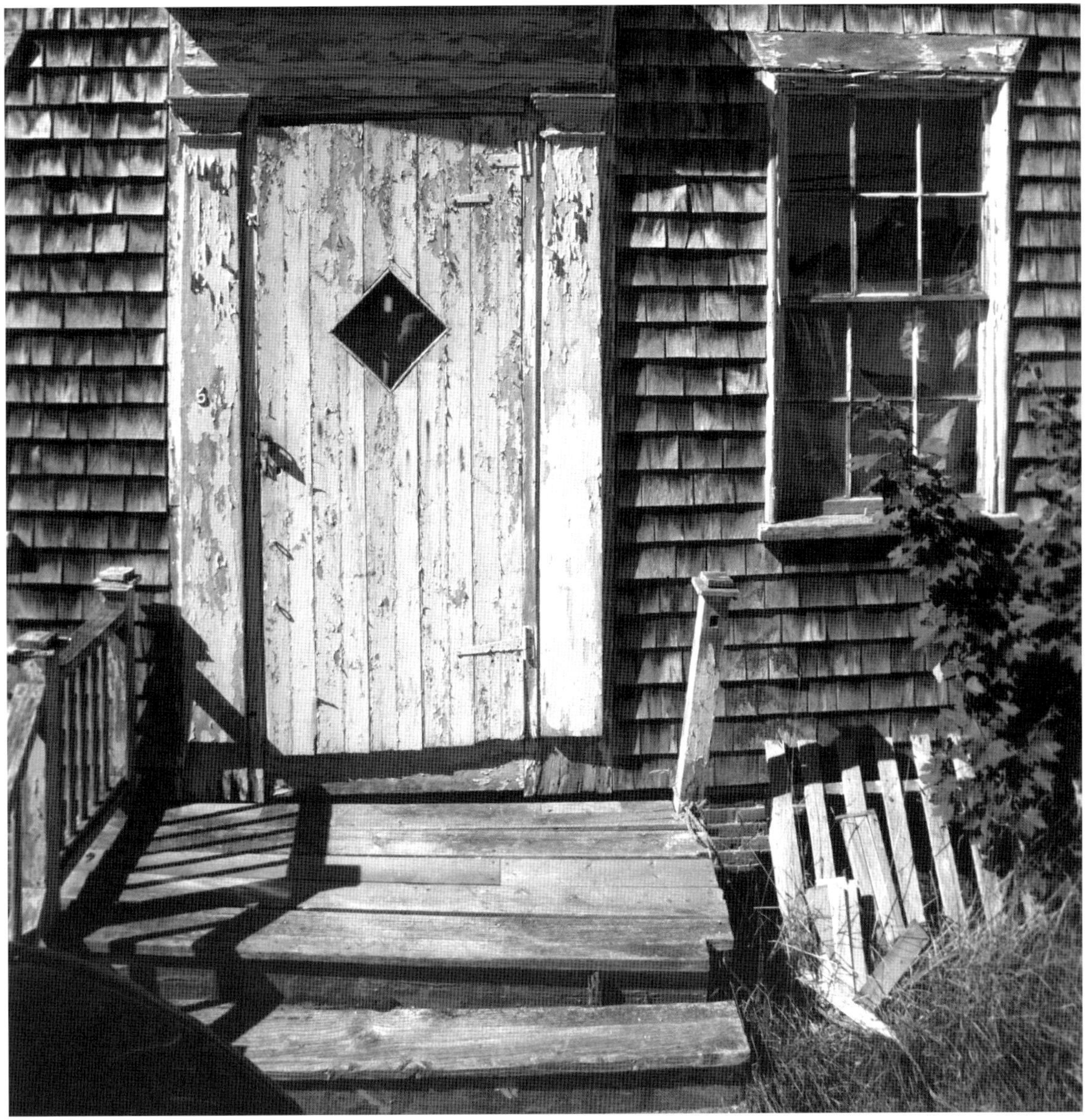

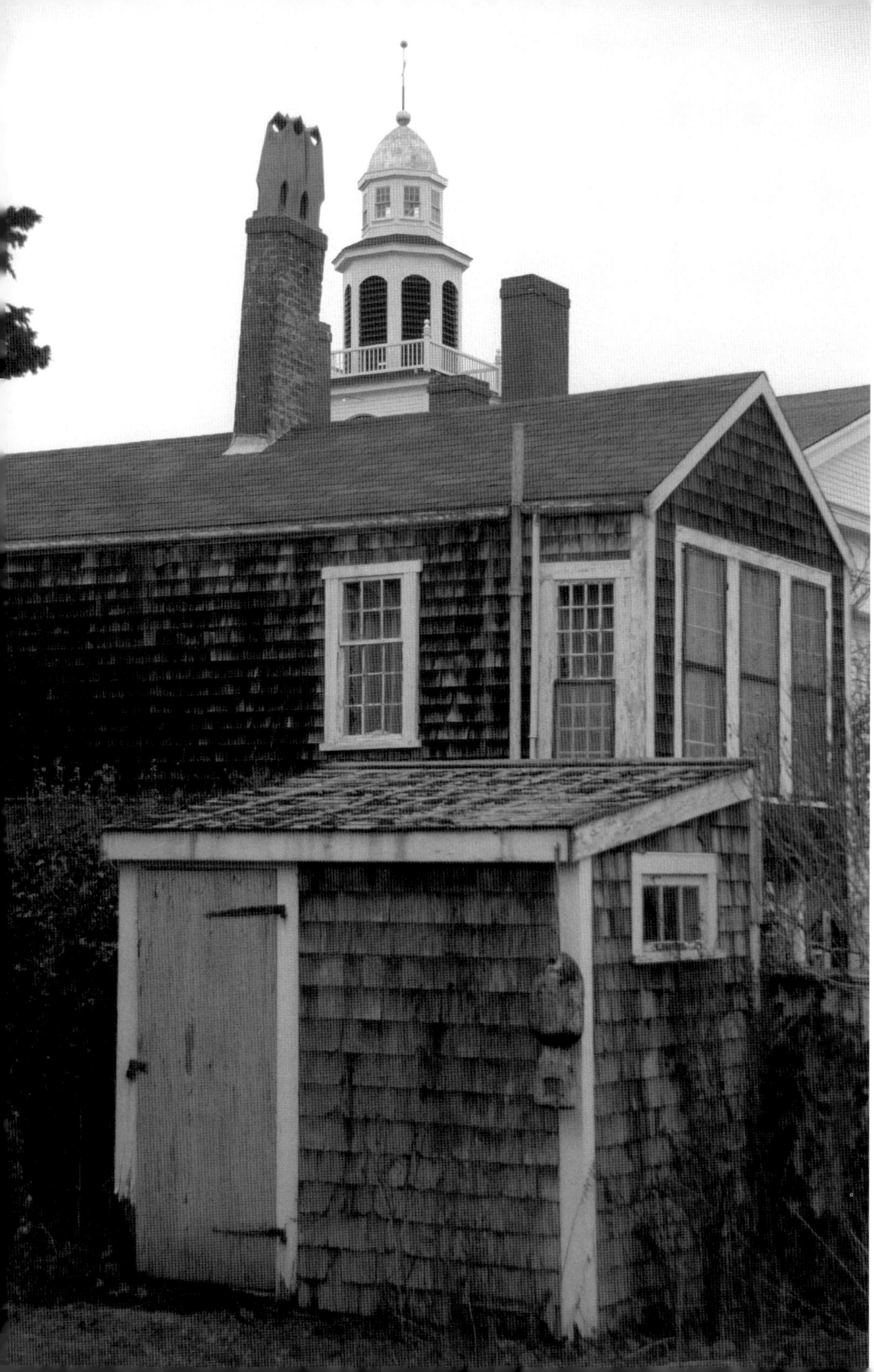

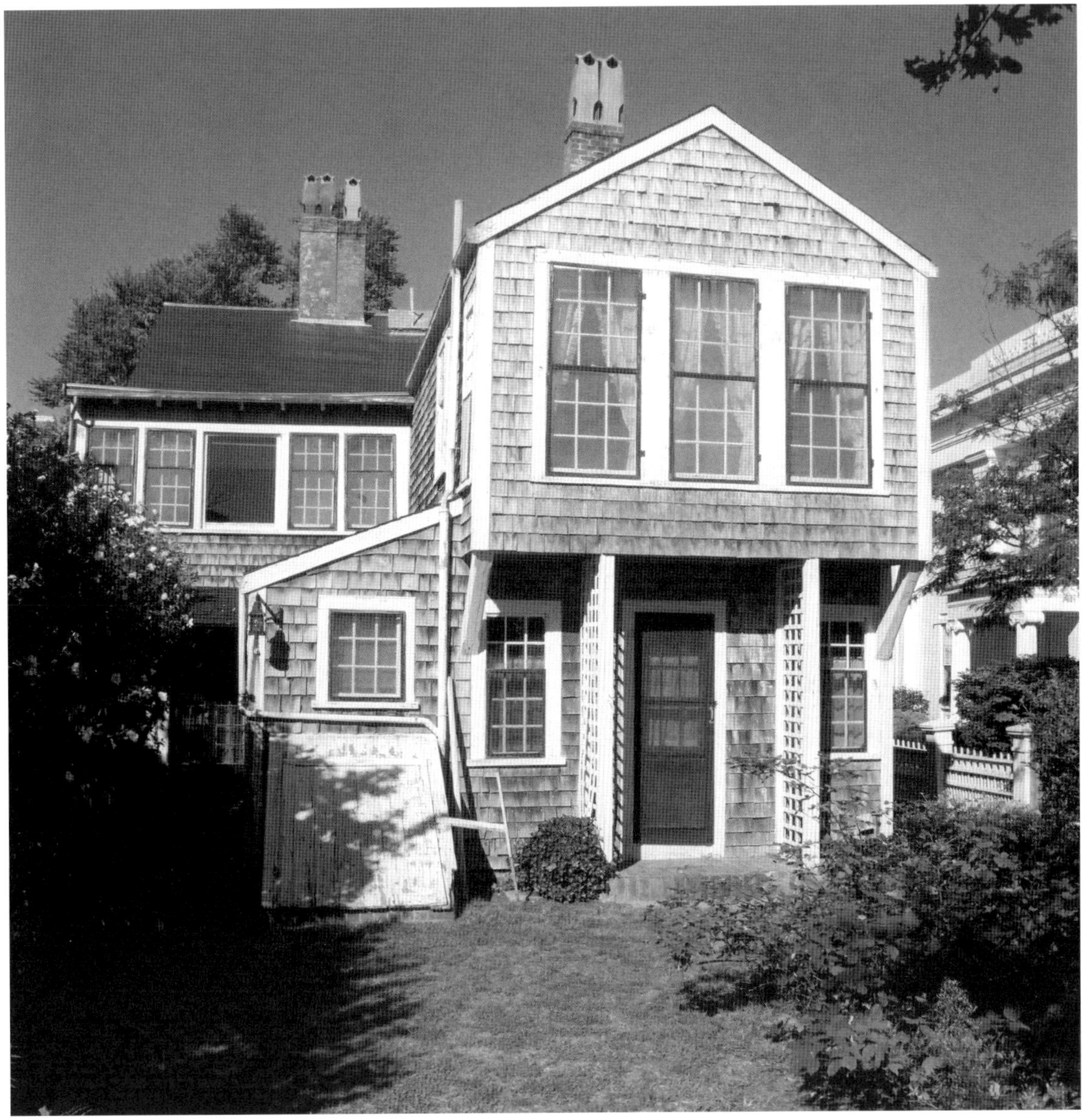

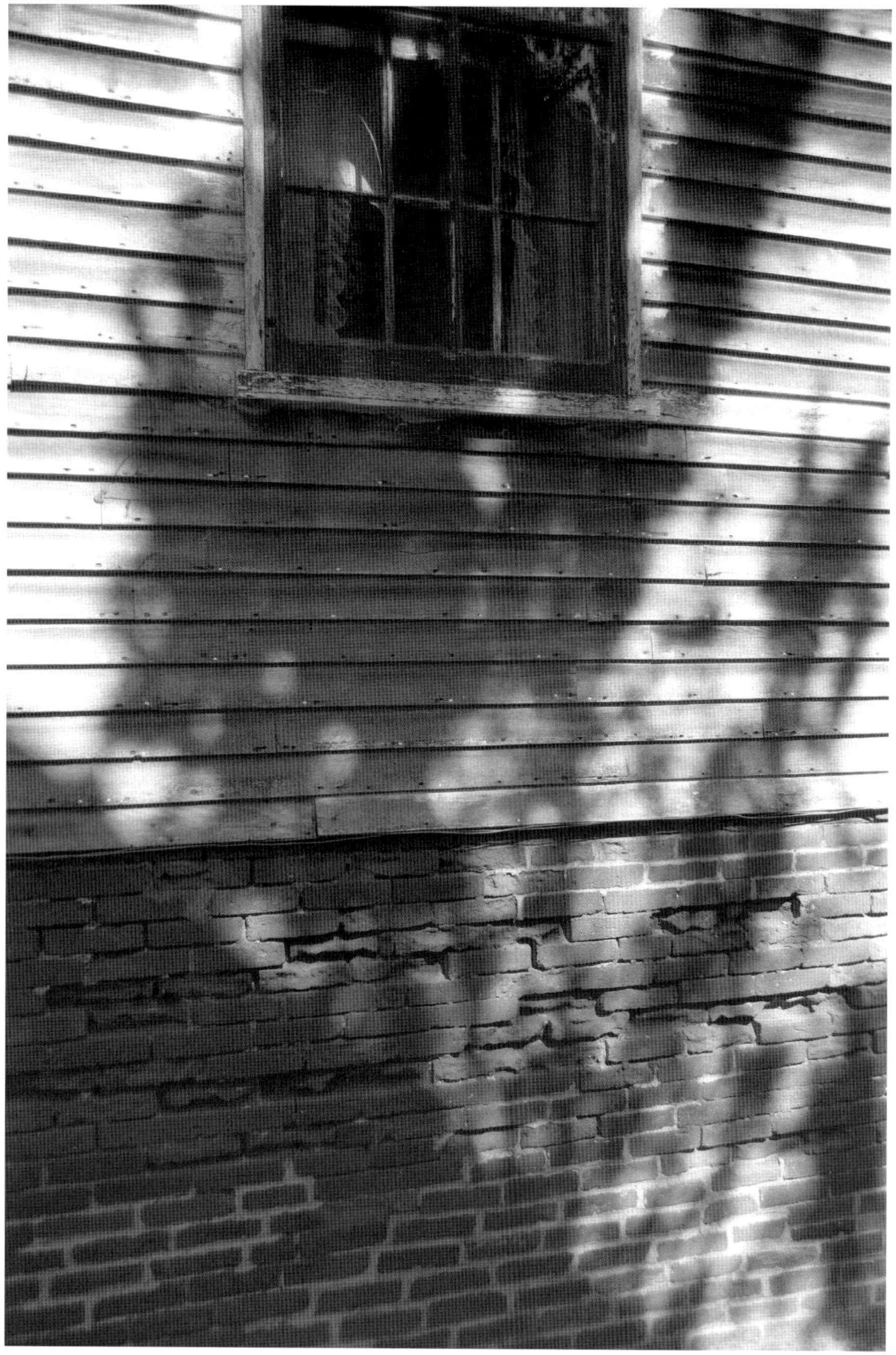

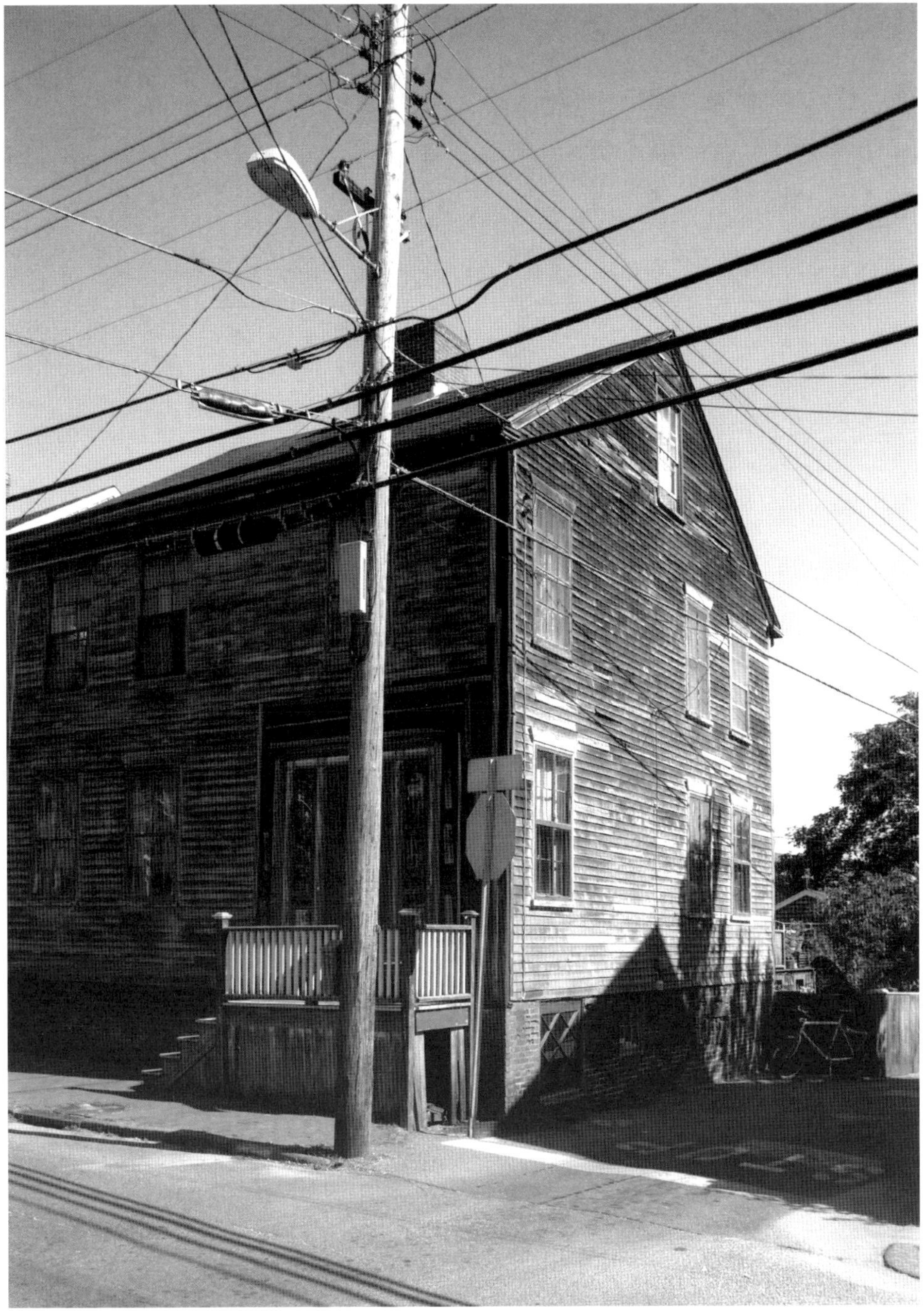

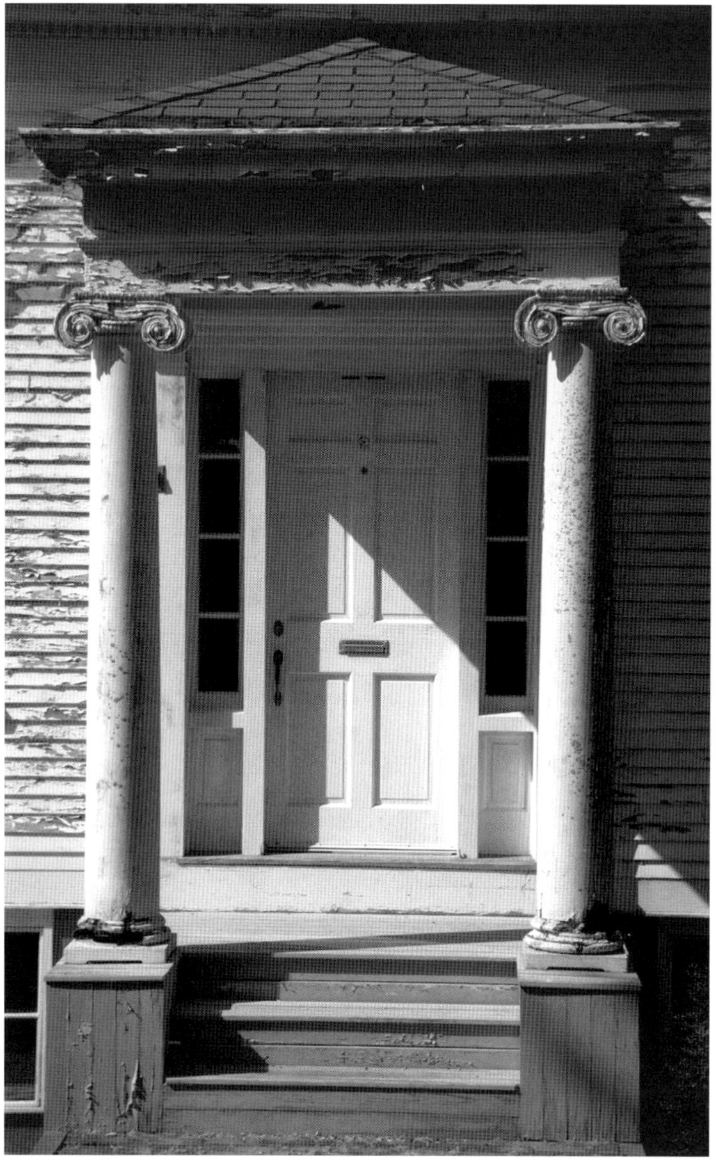

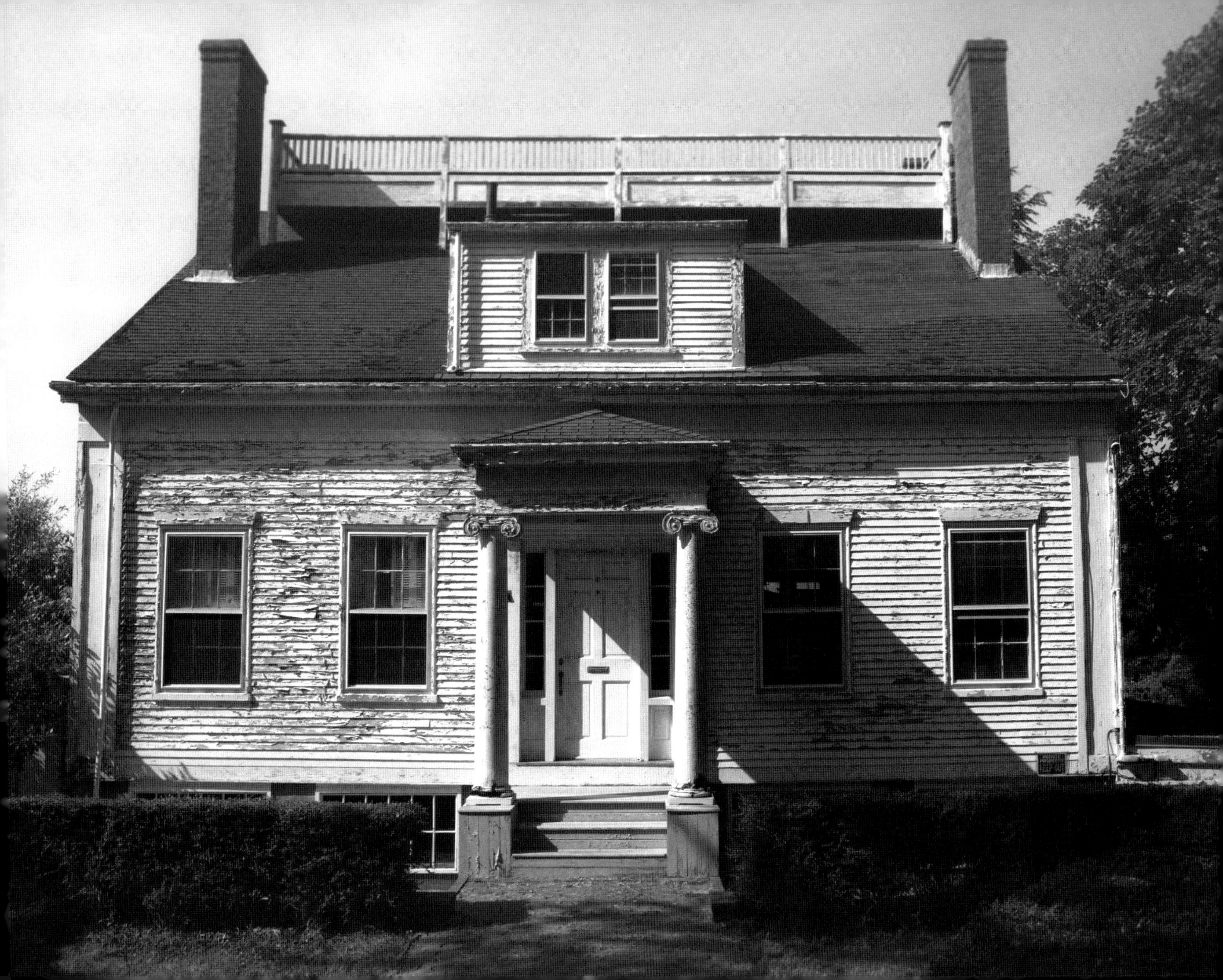

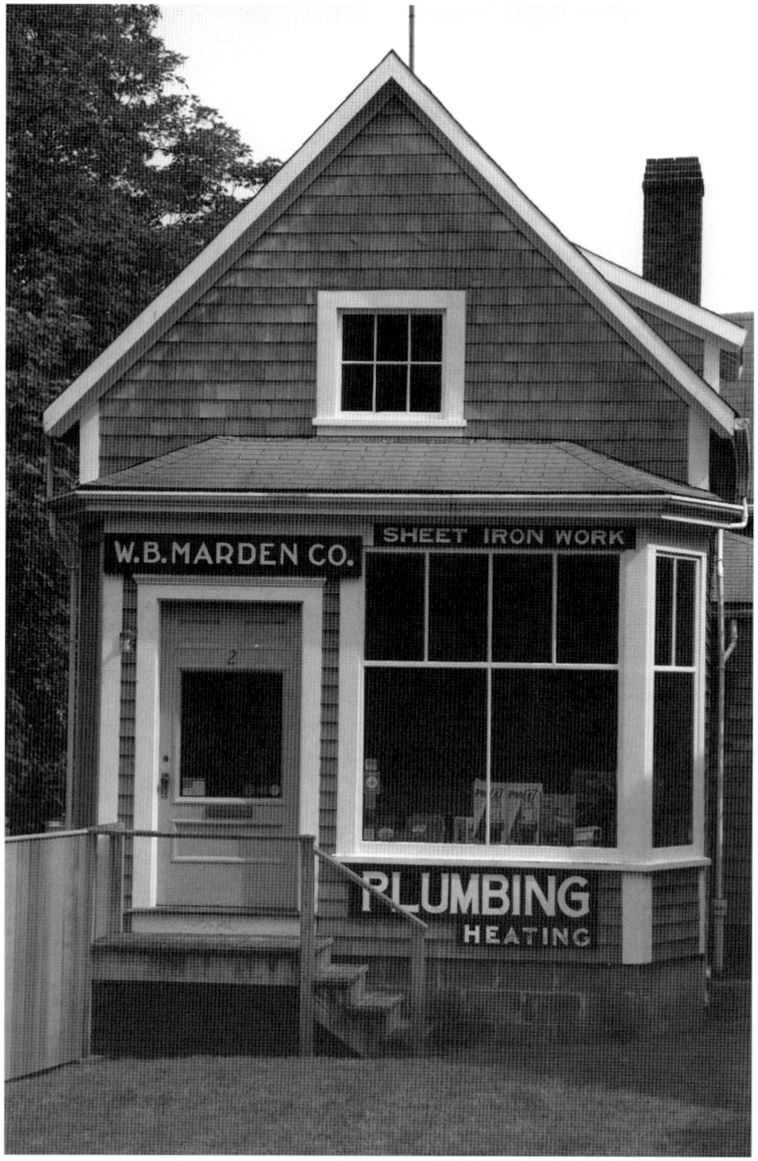
W.B. MARDEN CO.
SHEET IRON WORK
PLUMBING
HEATING

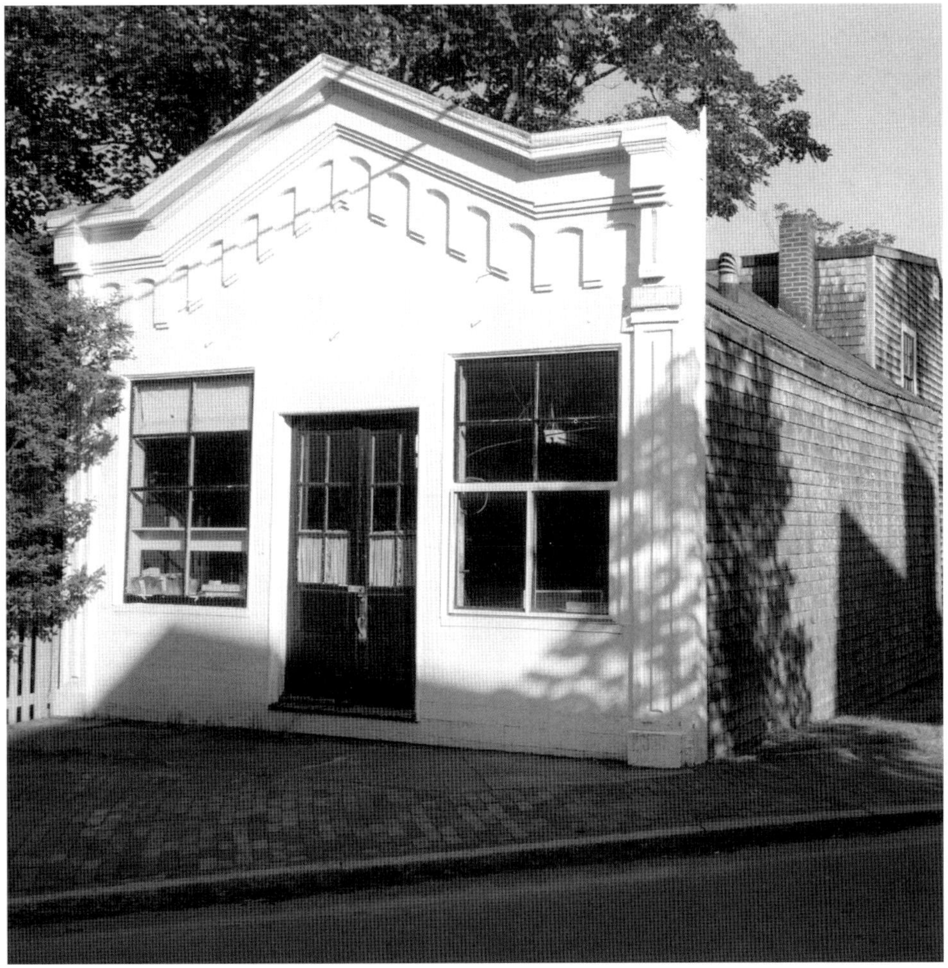

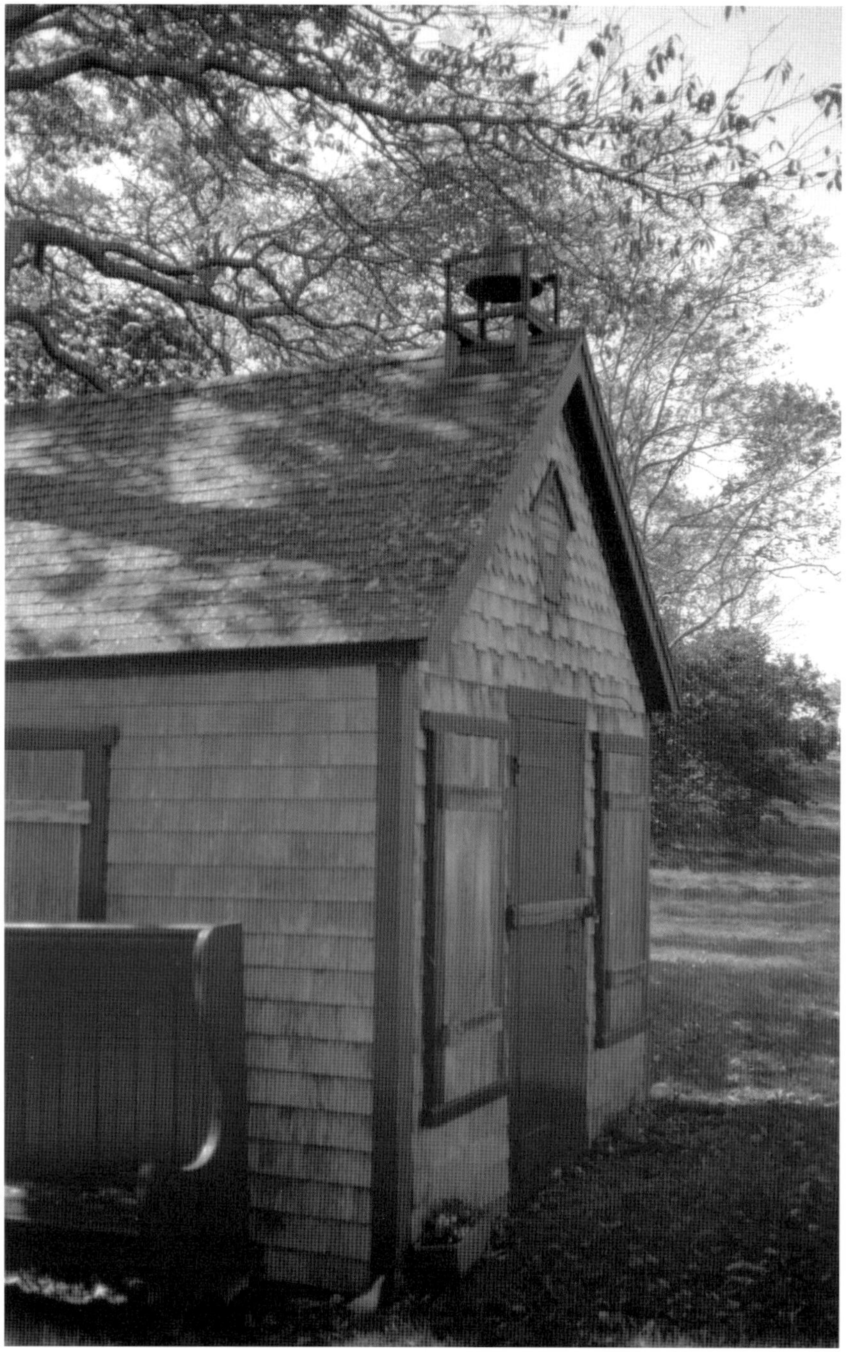

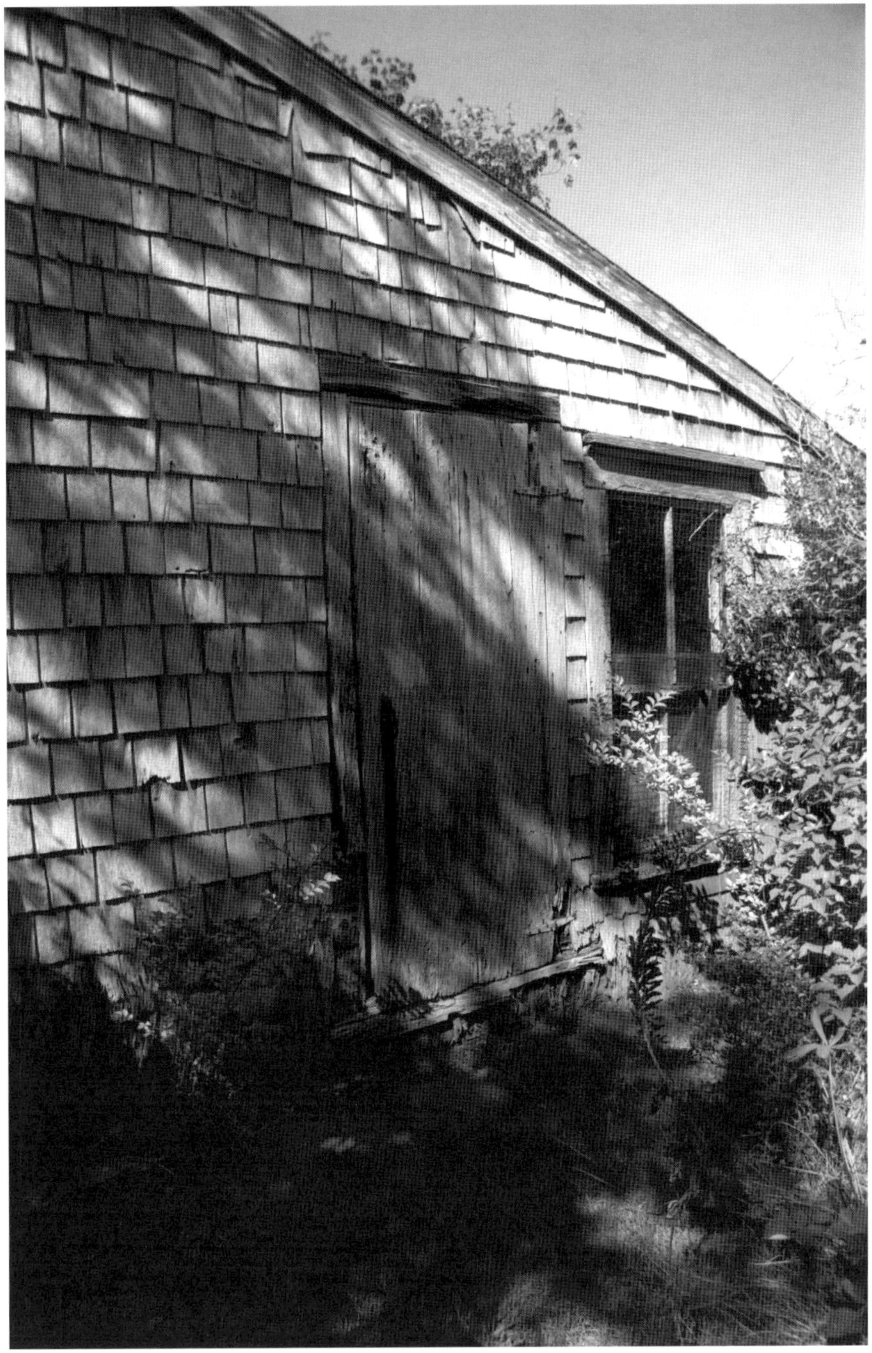

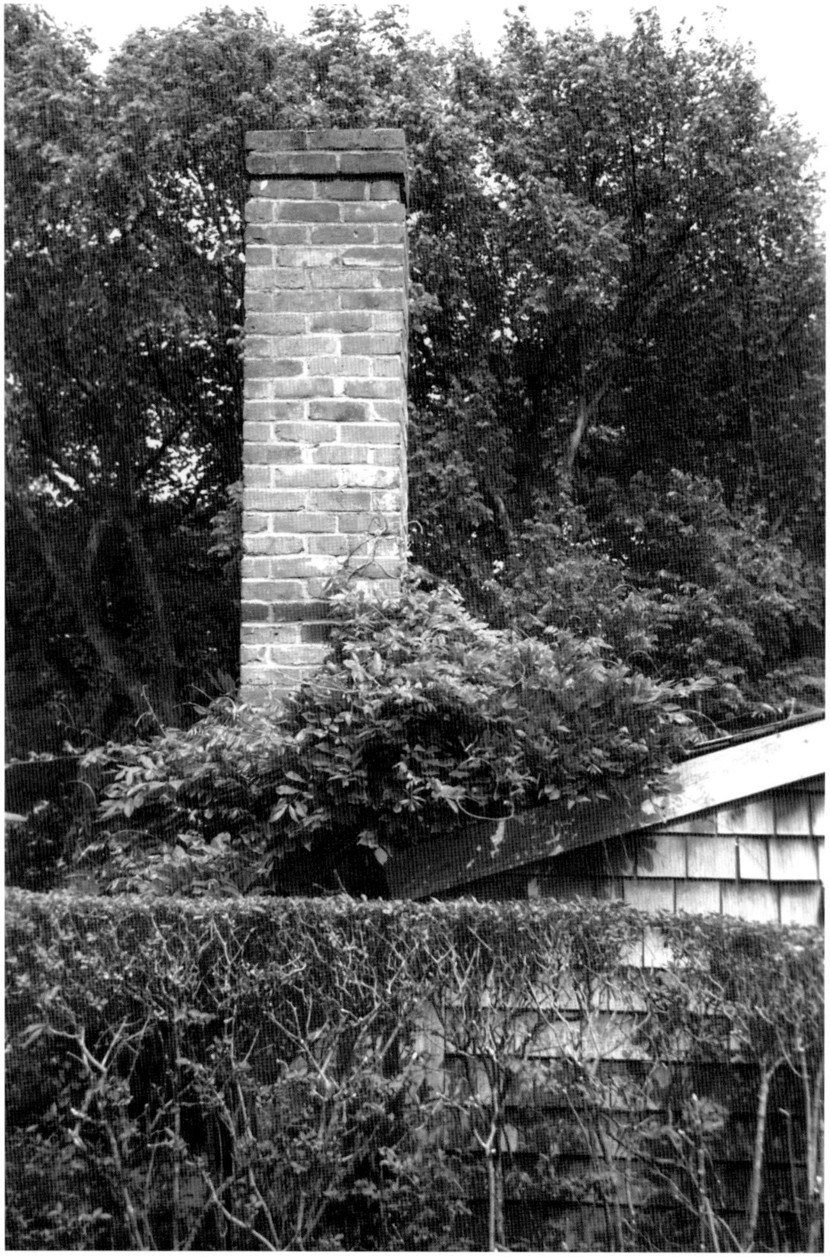

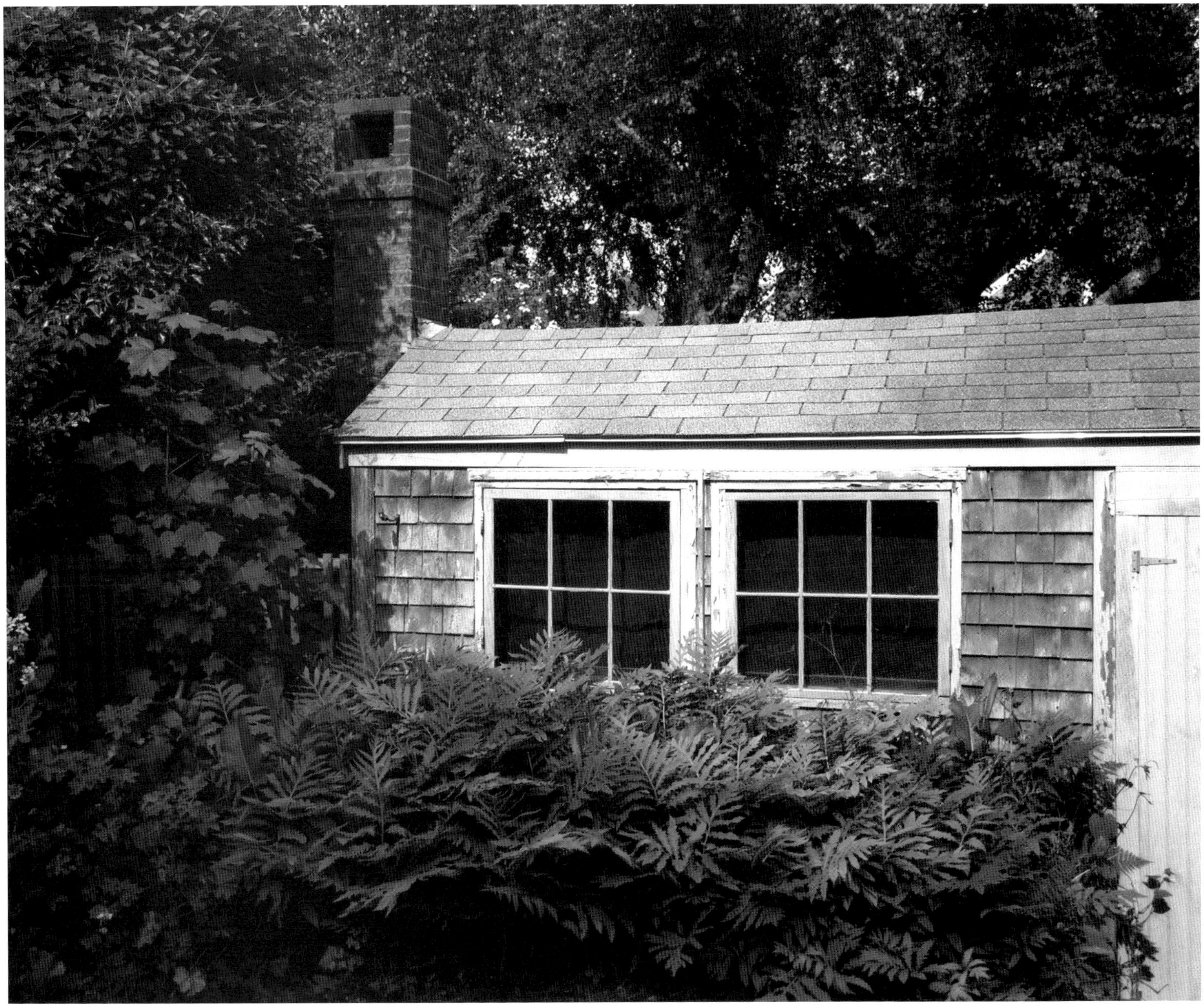

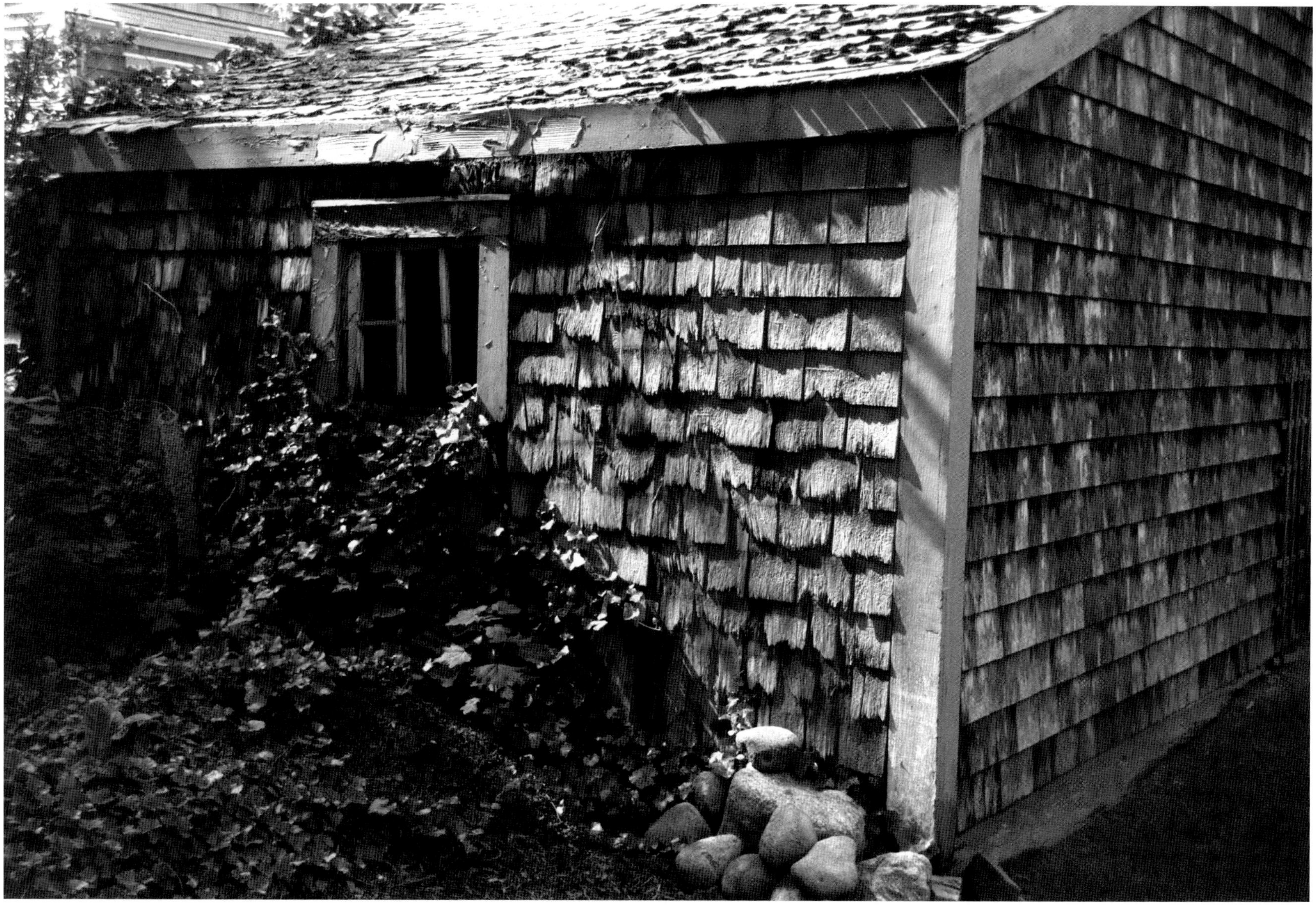

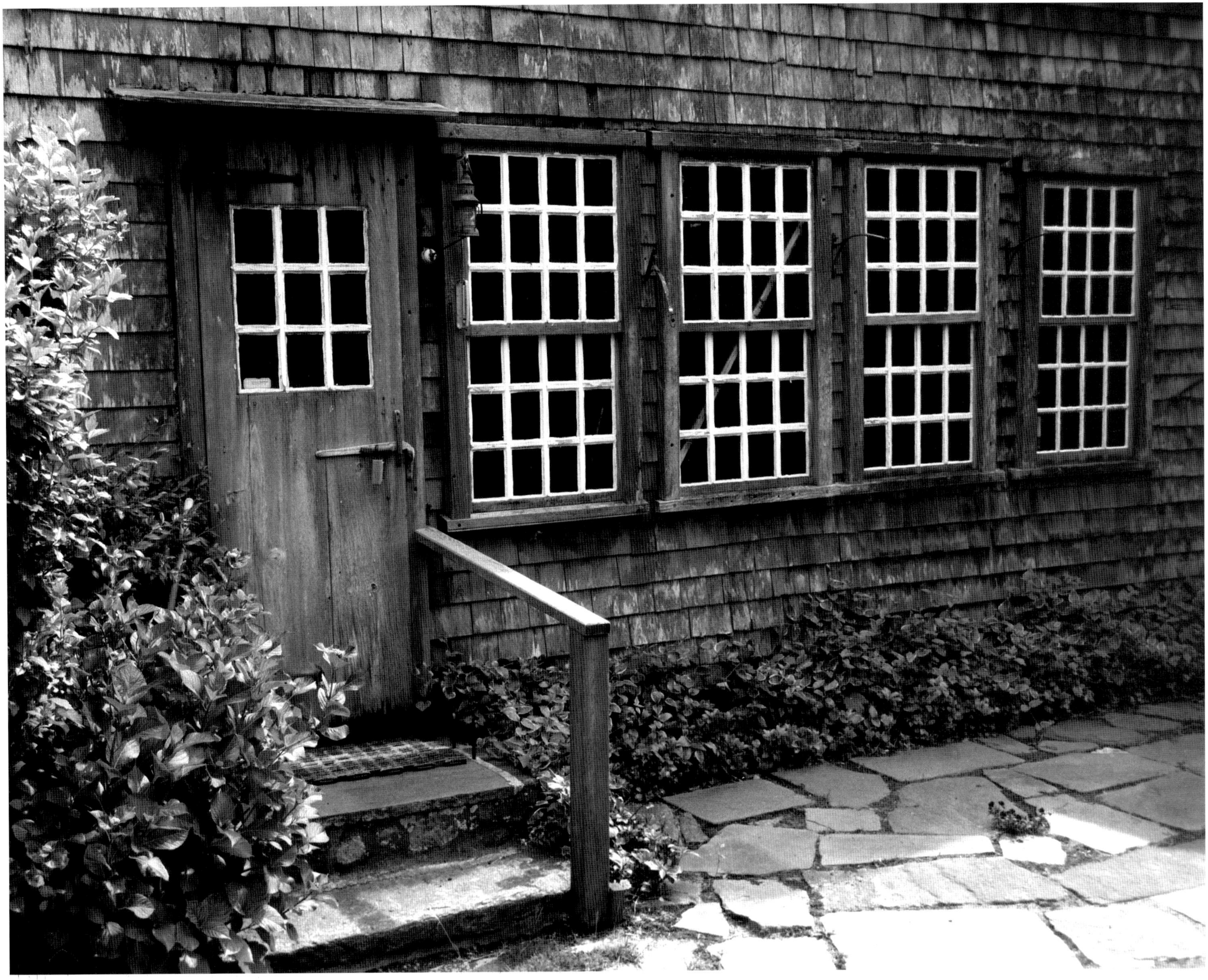

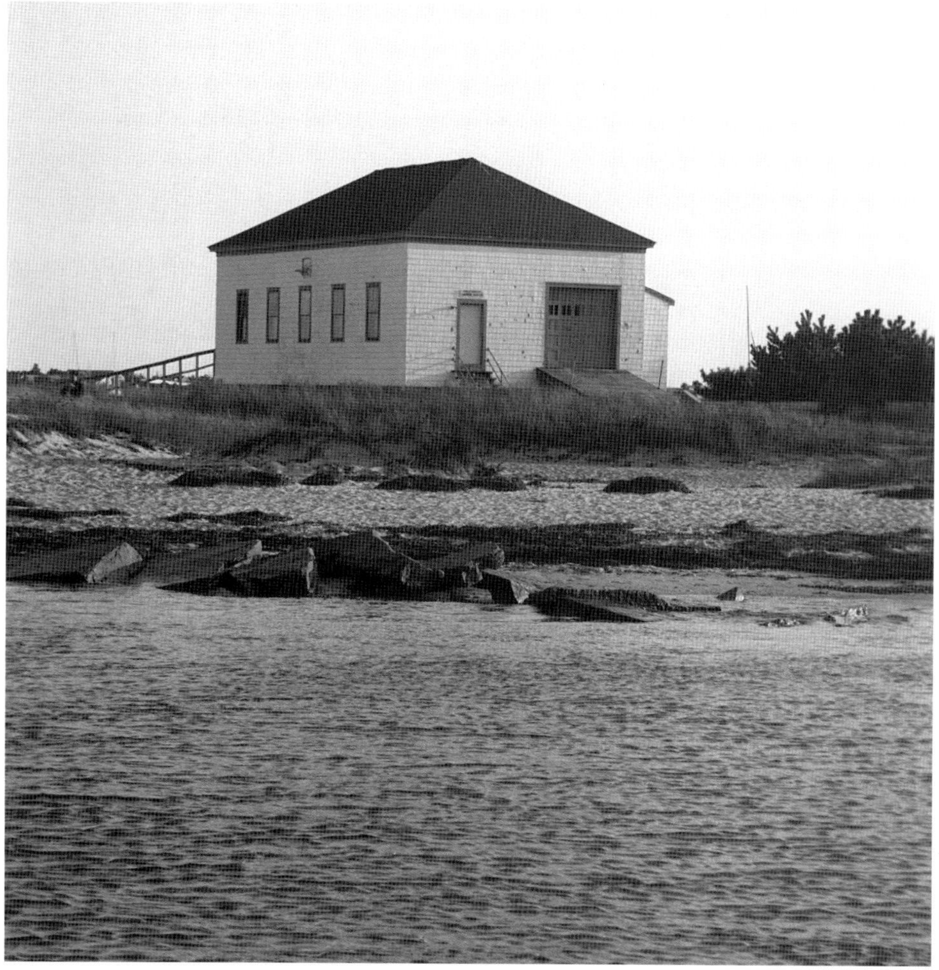

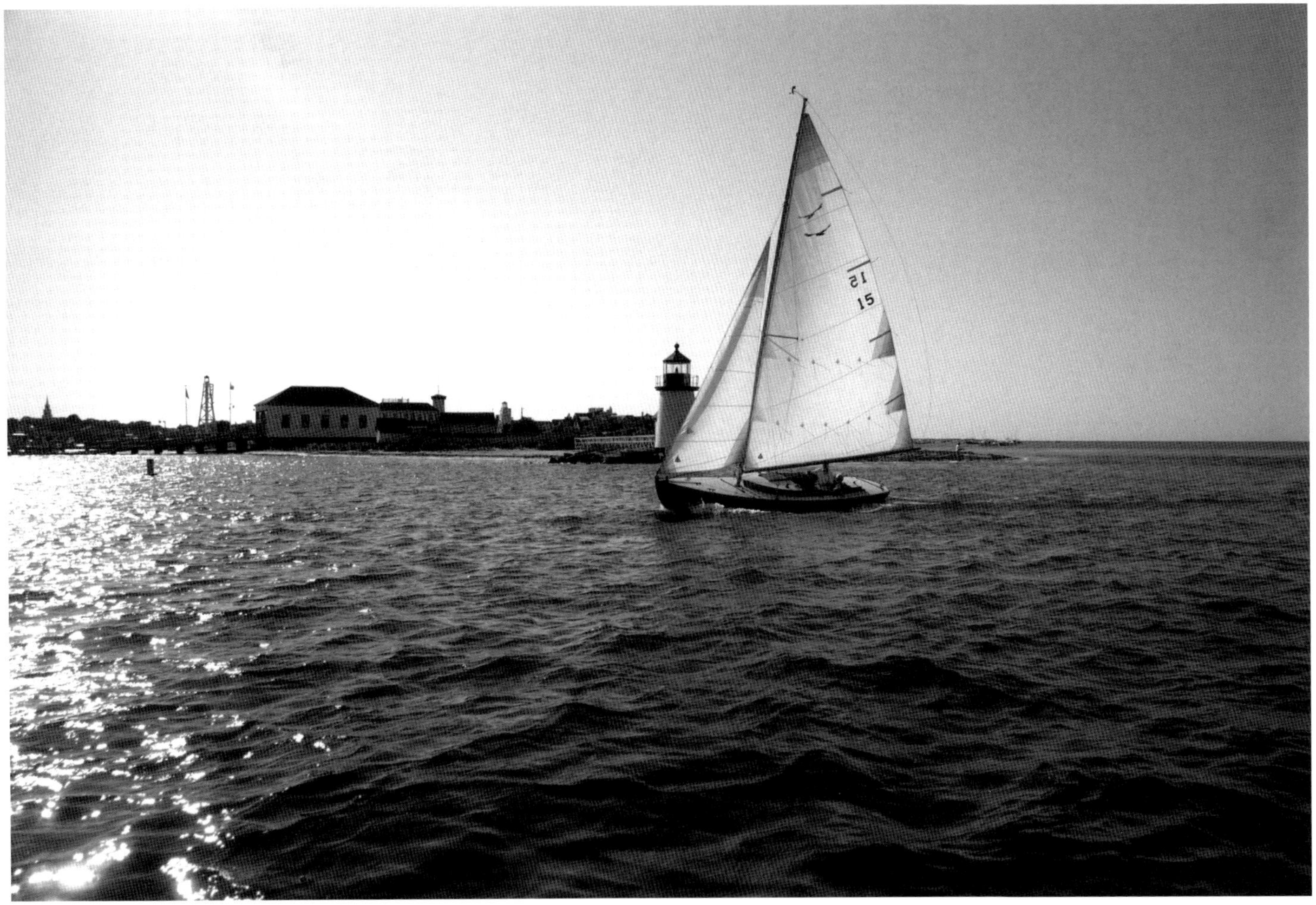
15
15

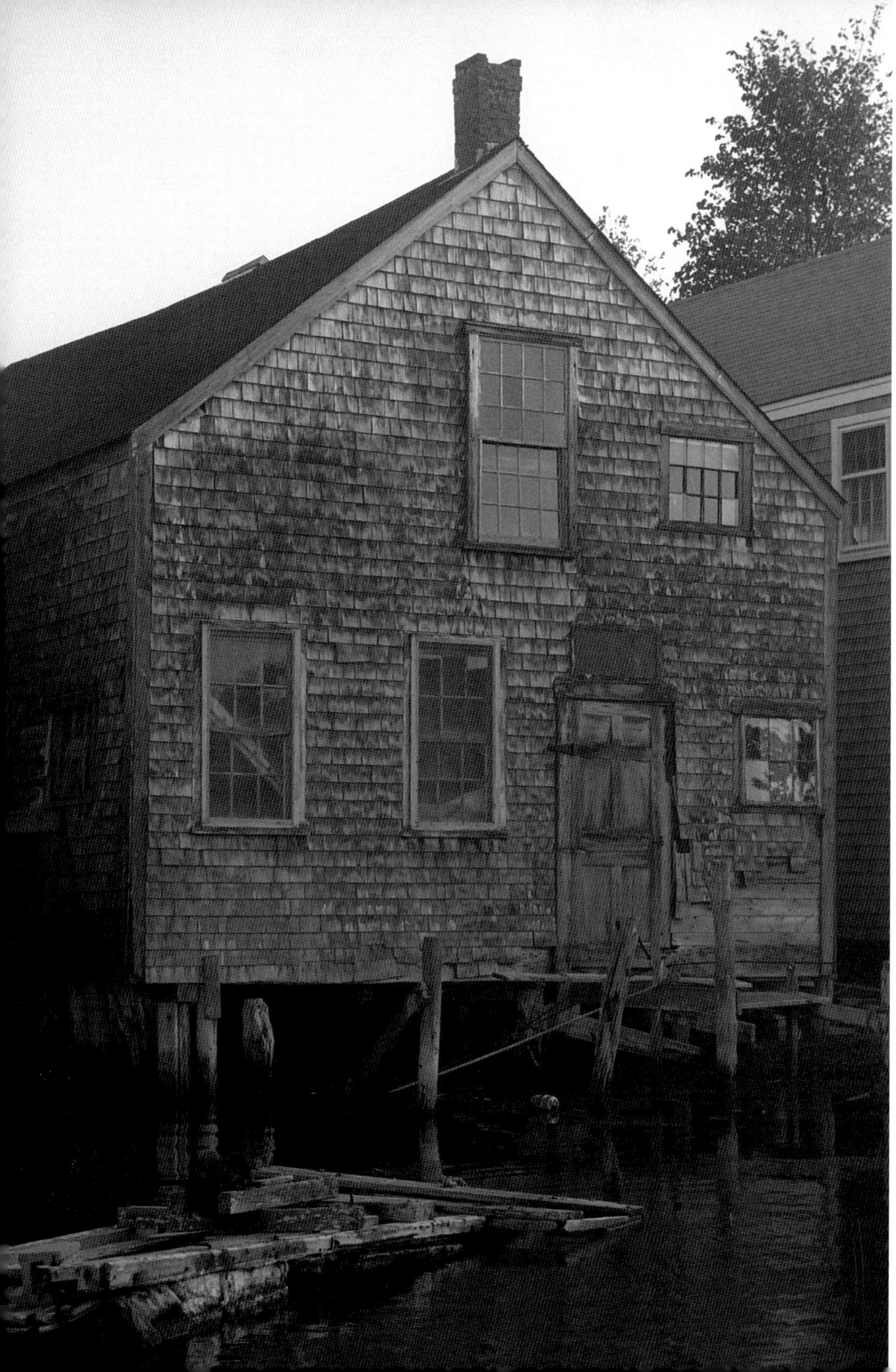

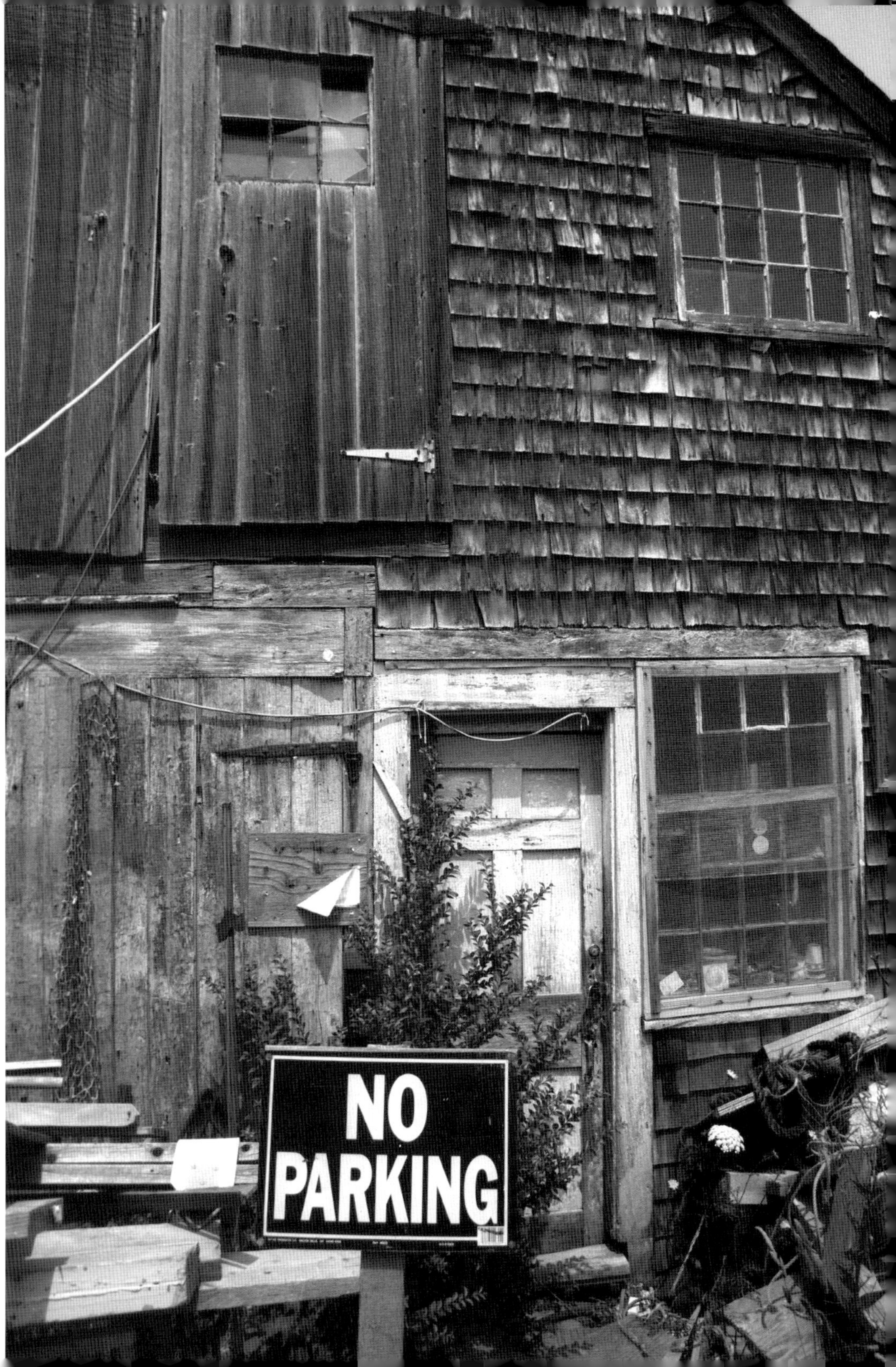
NO
PARKING

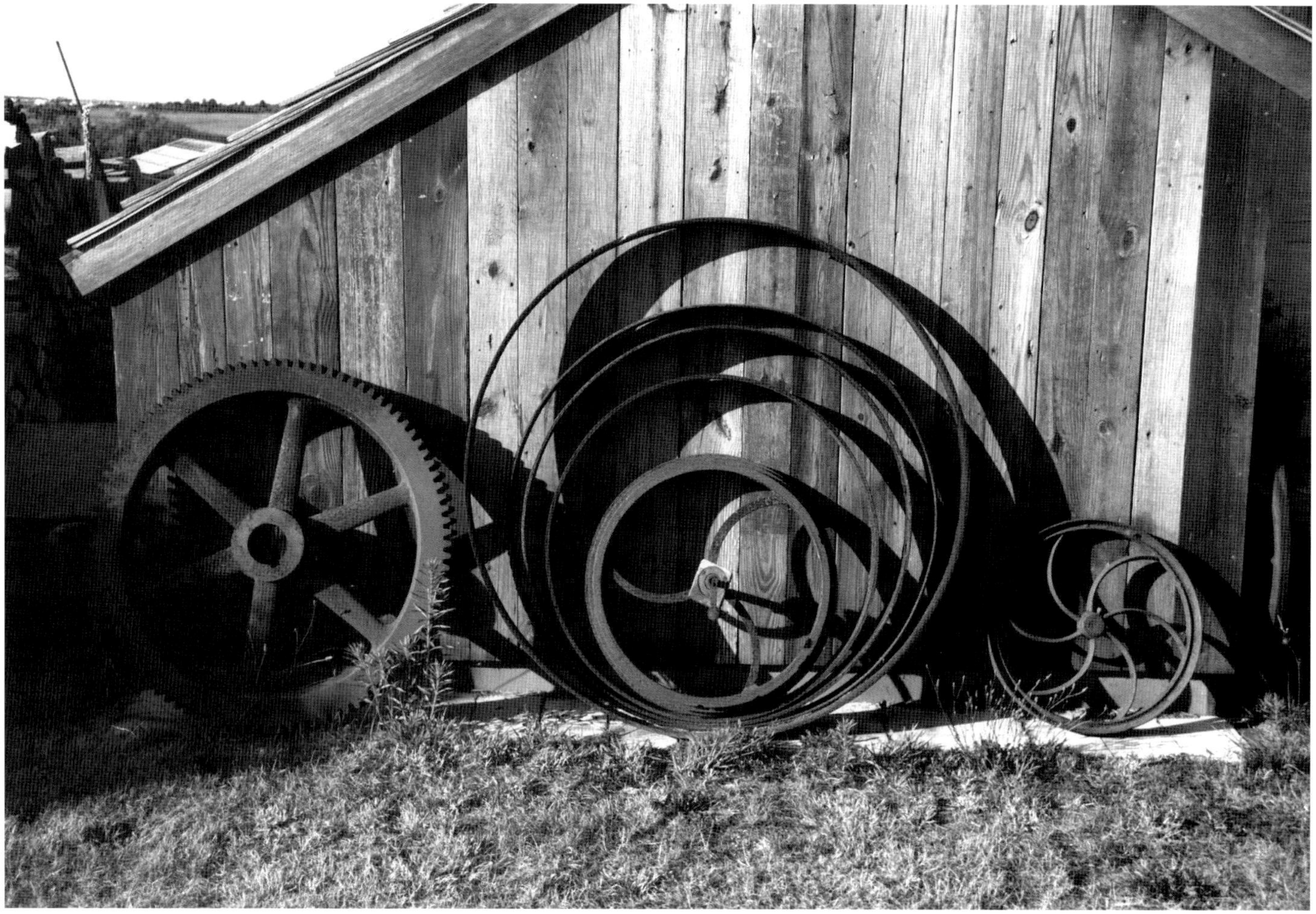

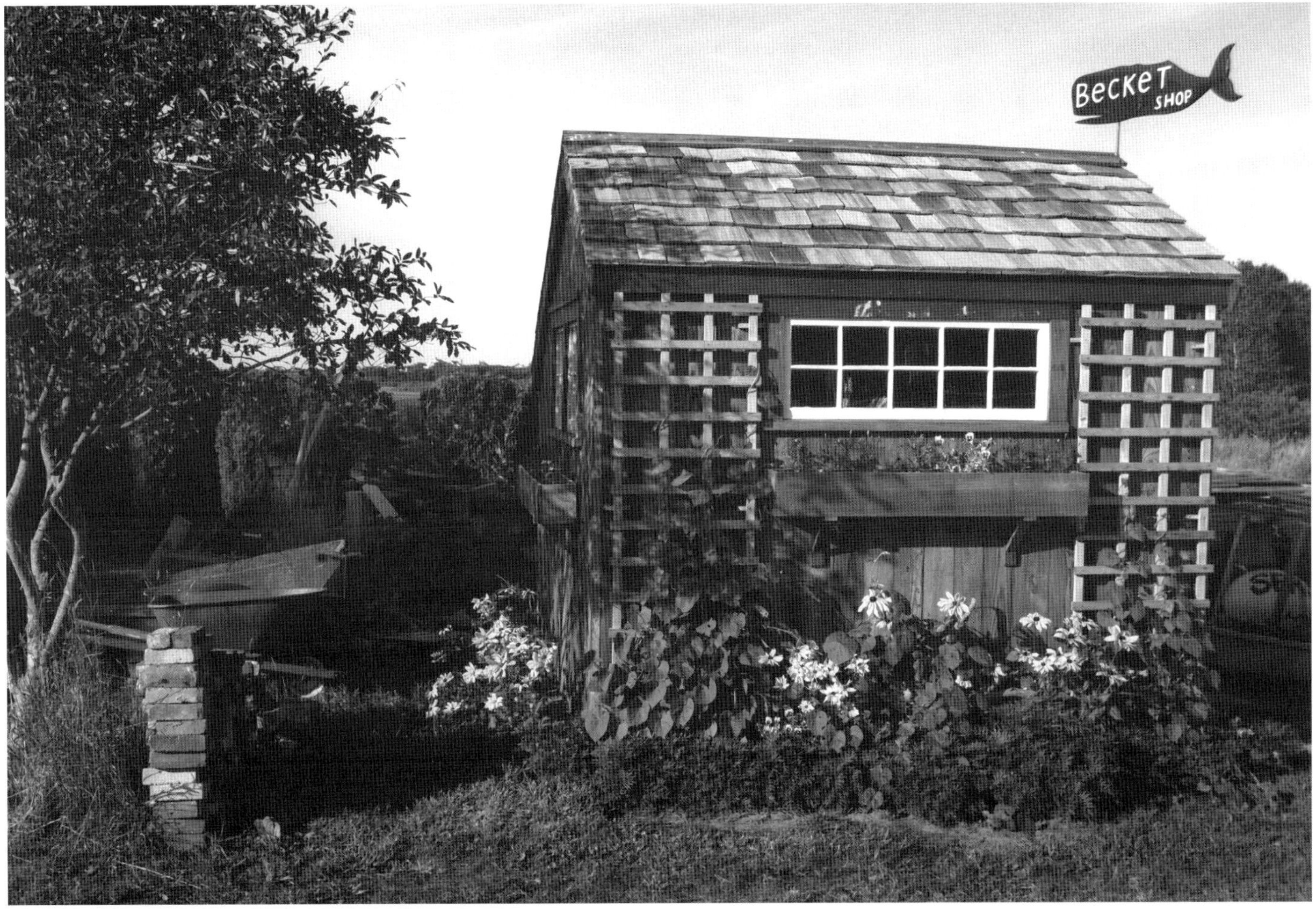
Becket
SHOP

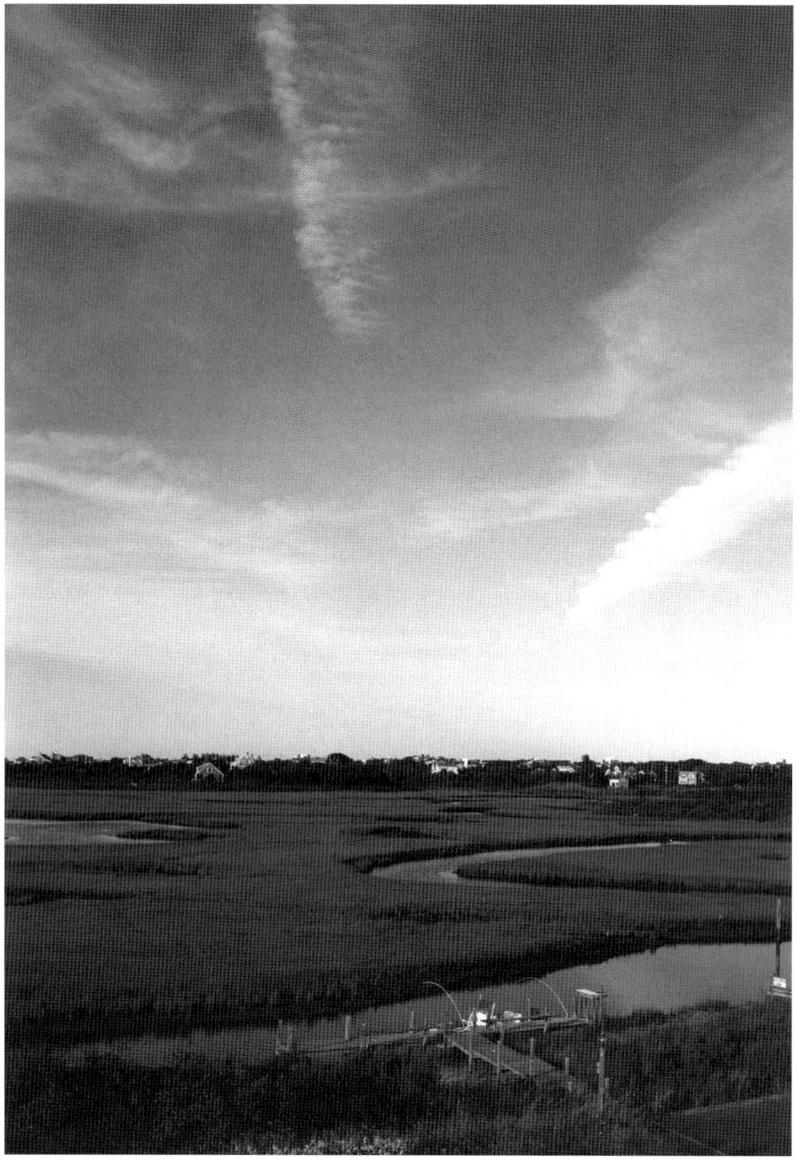

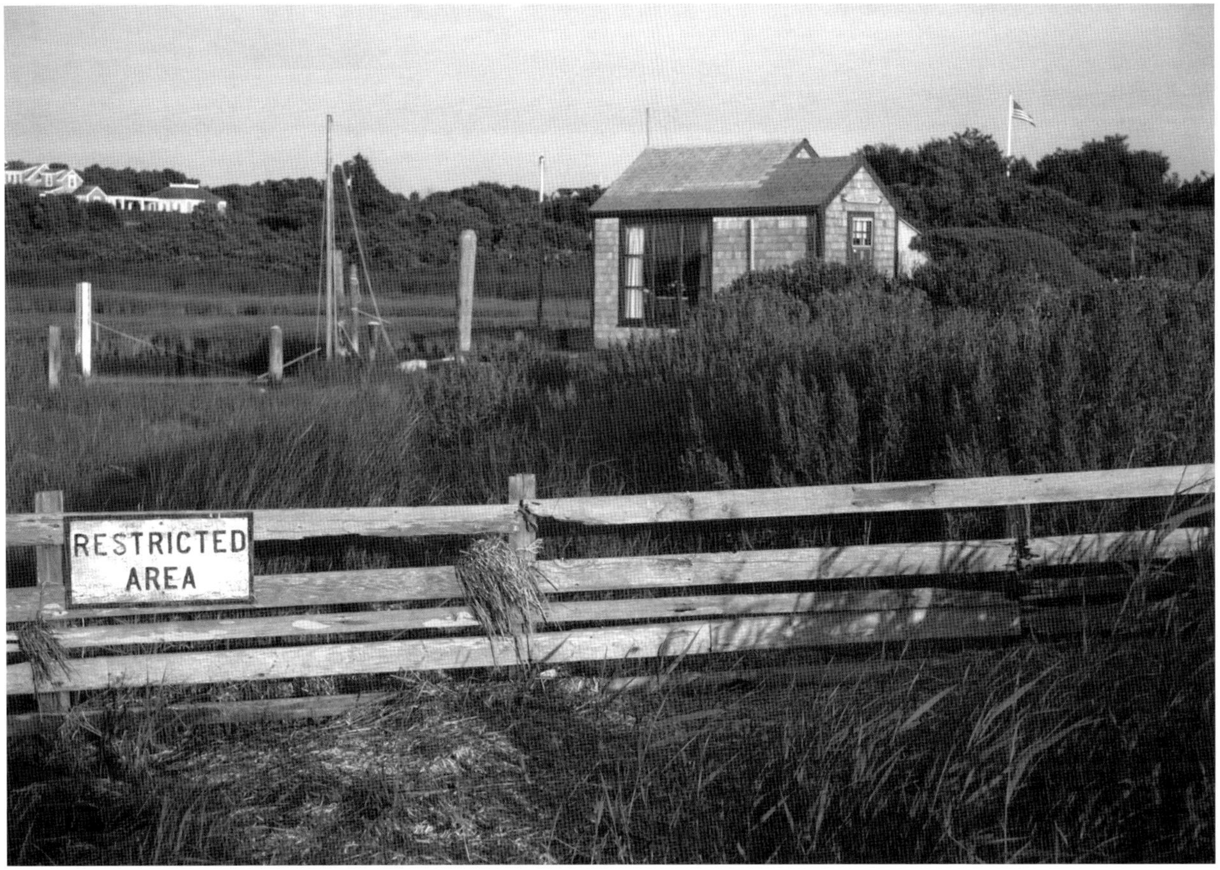
RESTRICTED
AREA

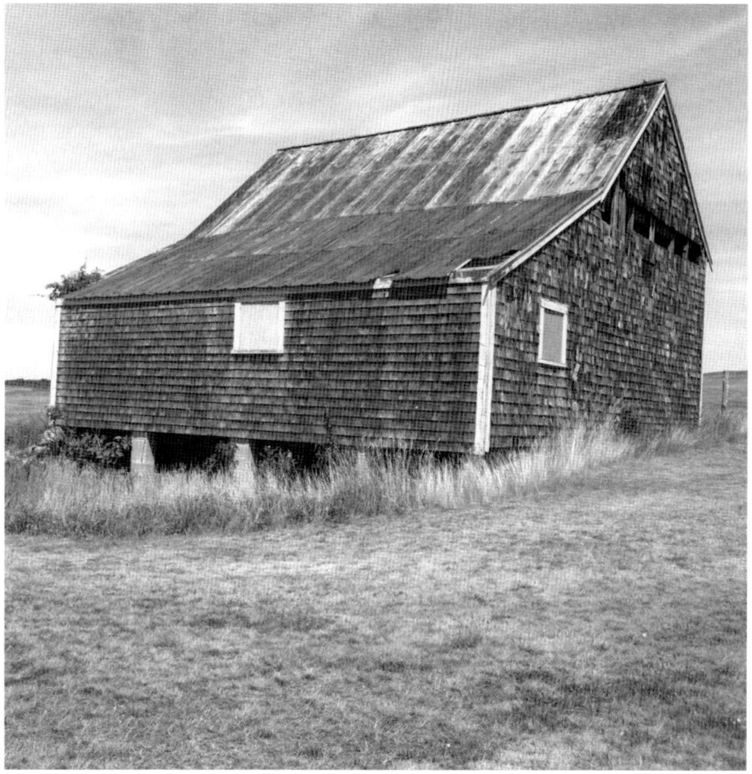

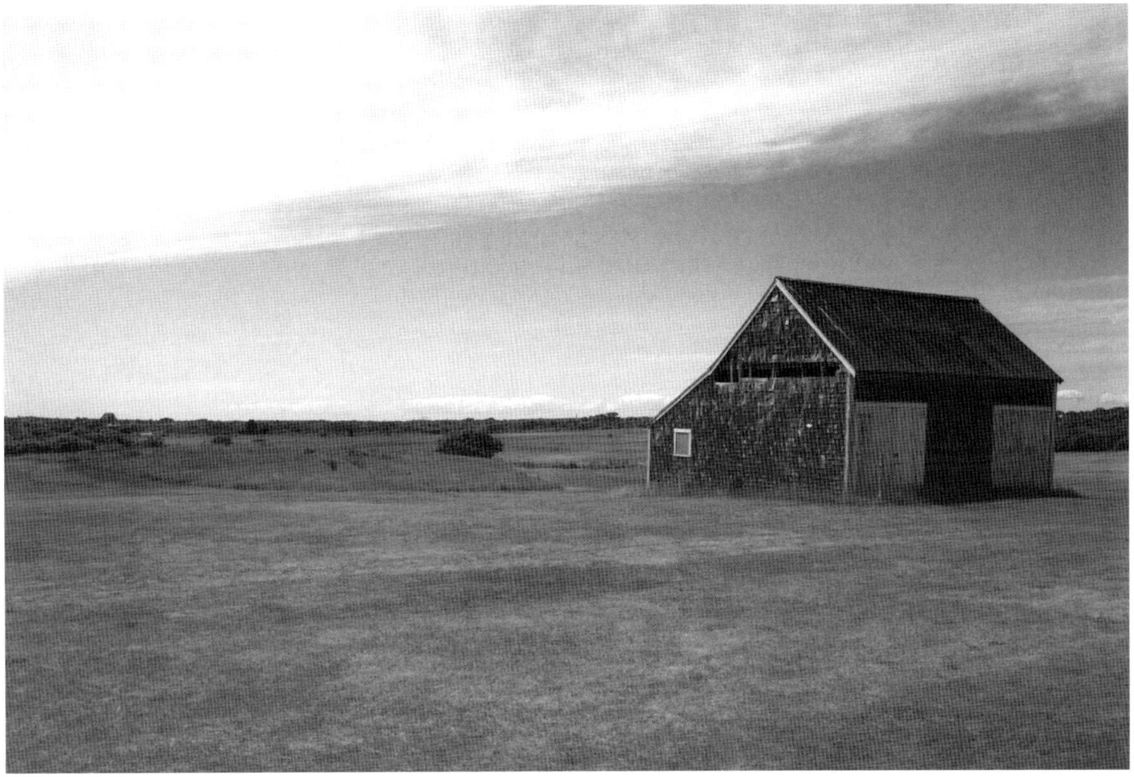

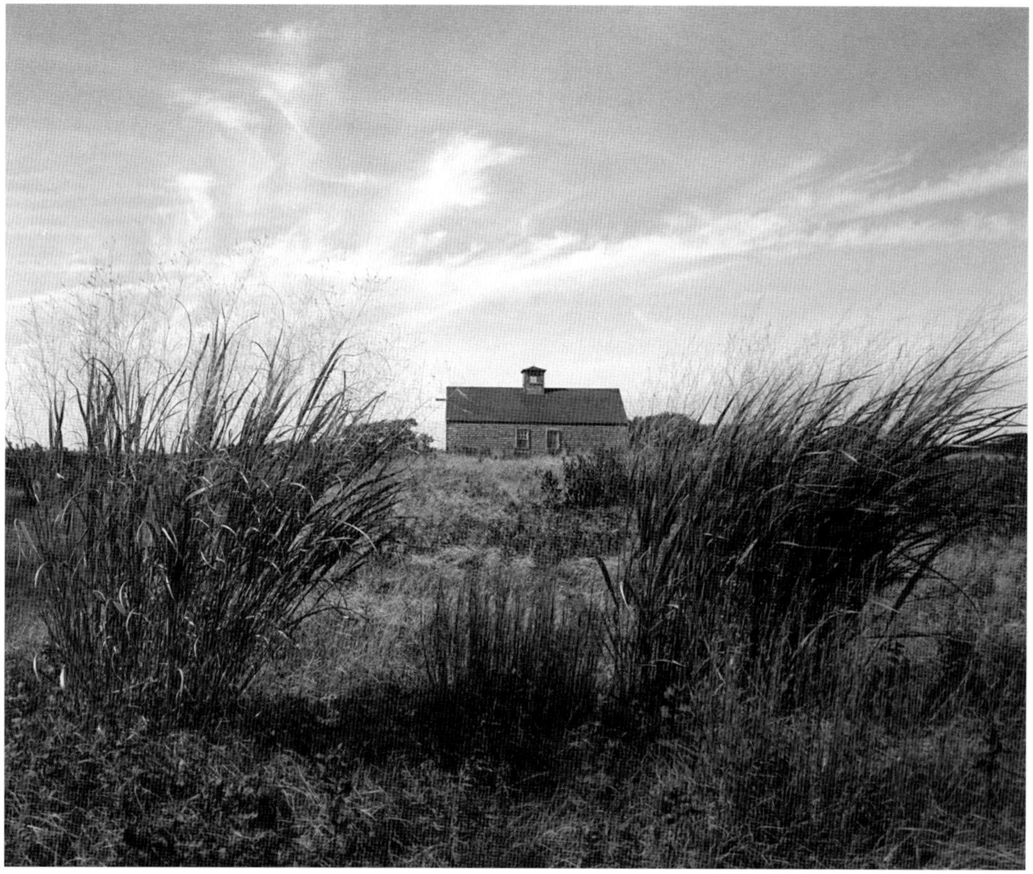

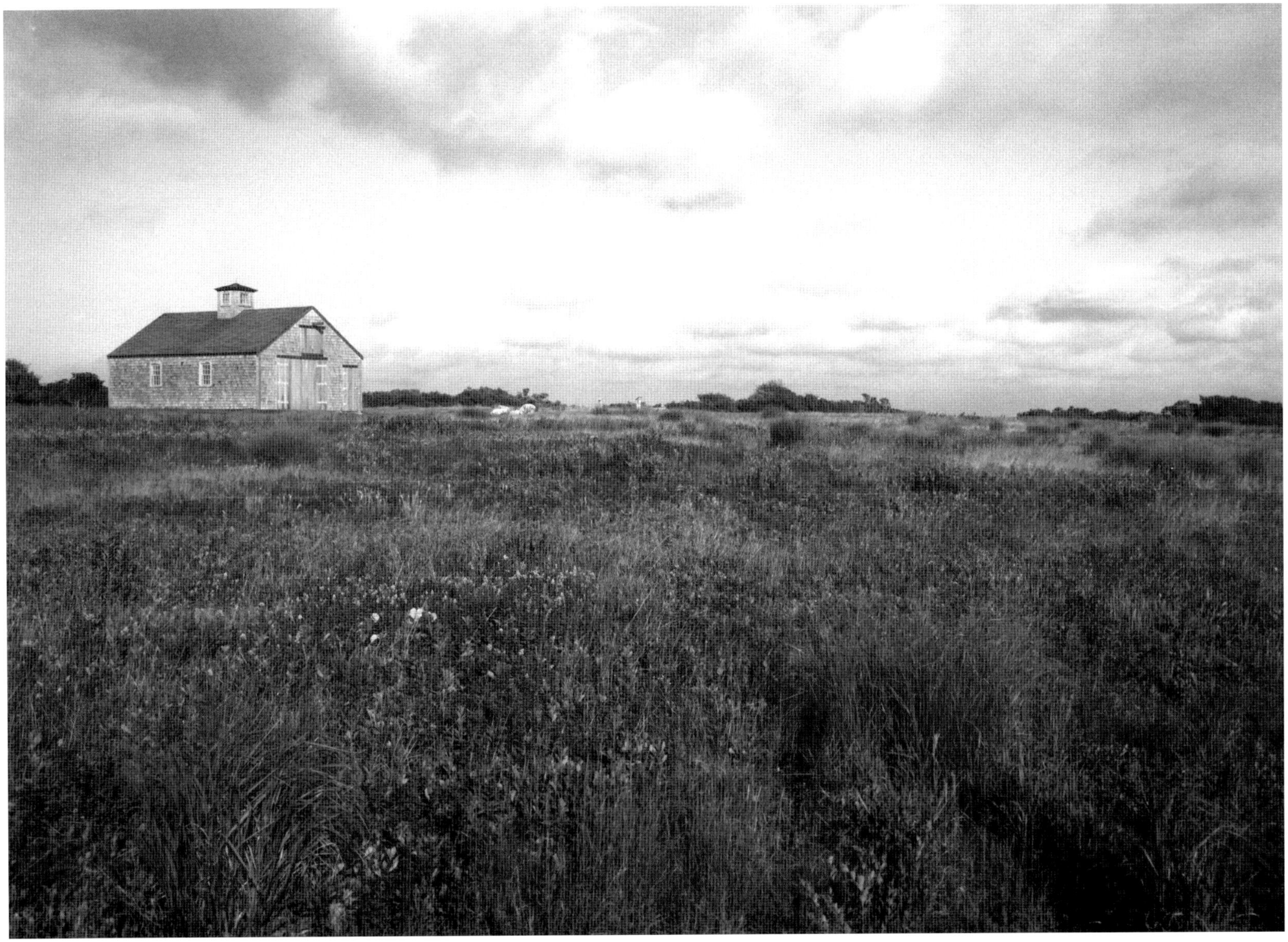

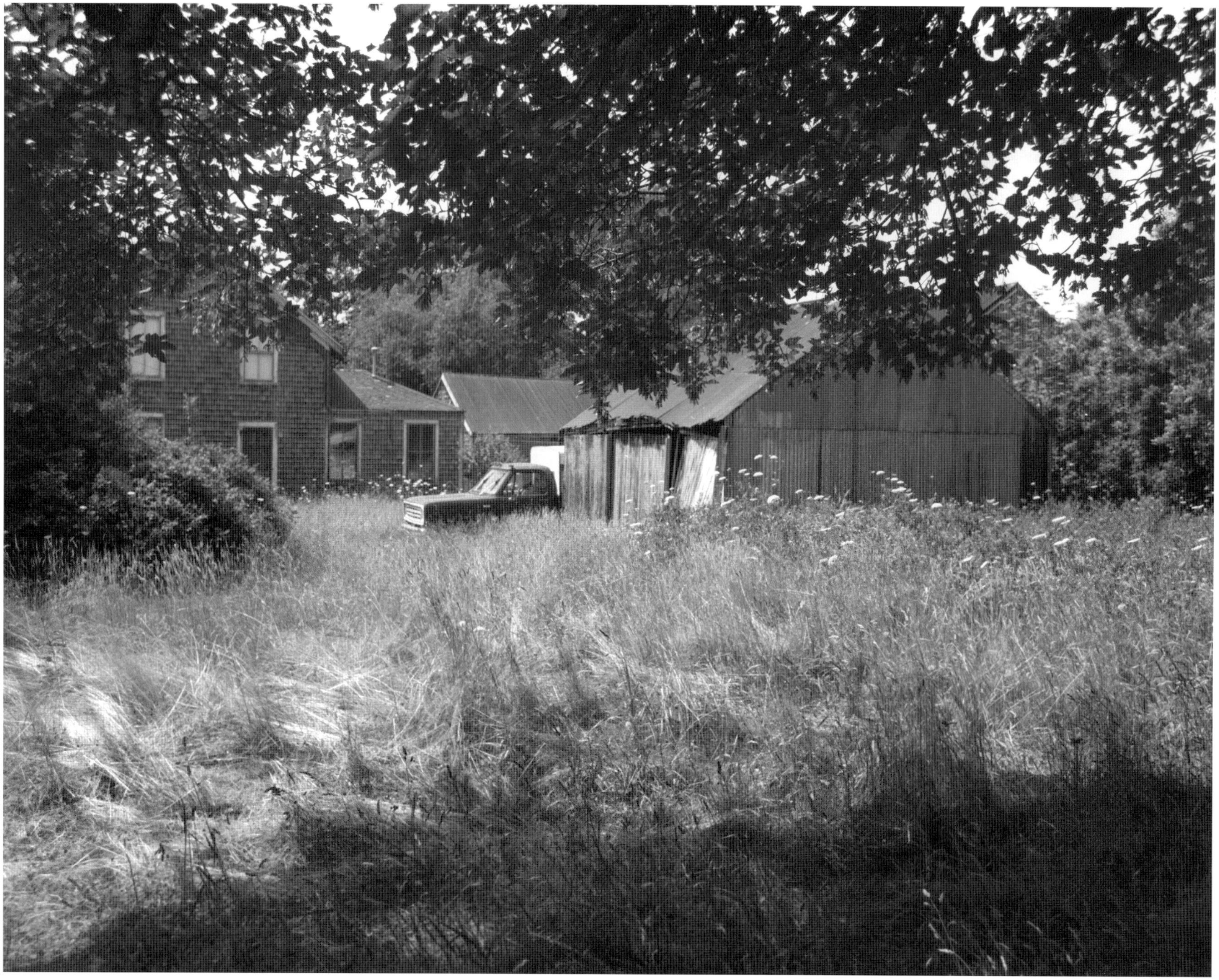

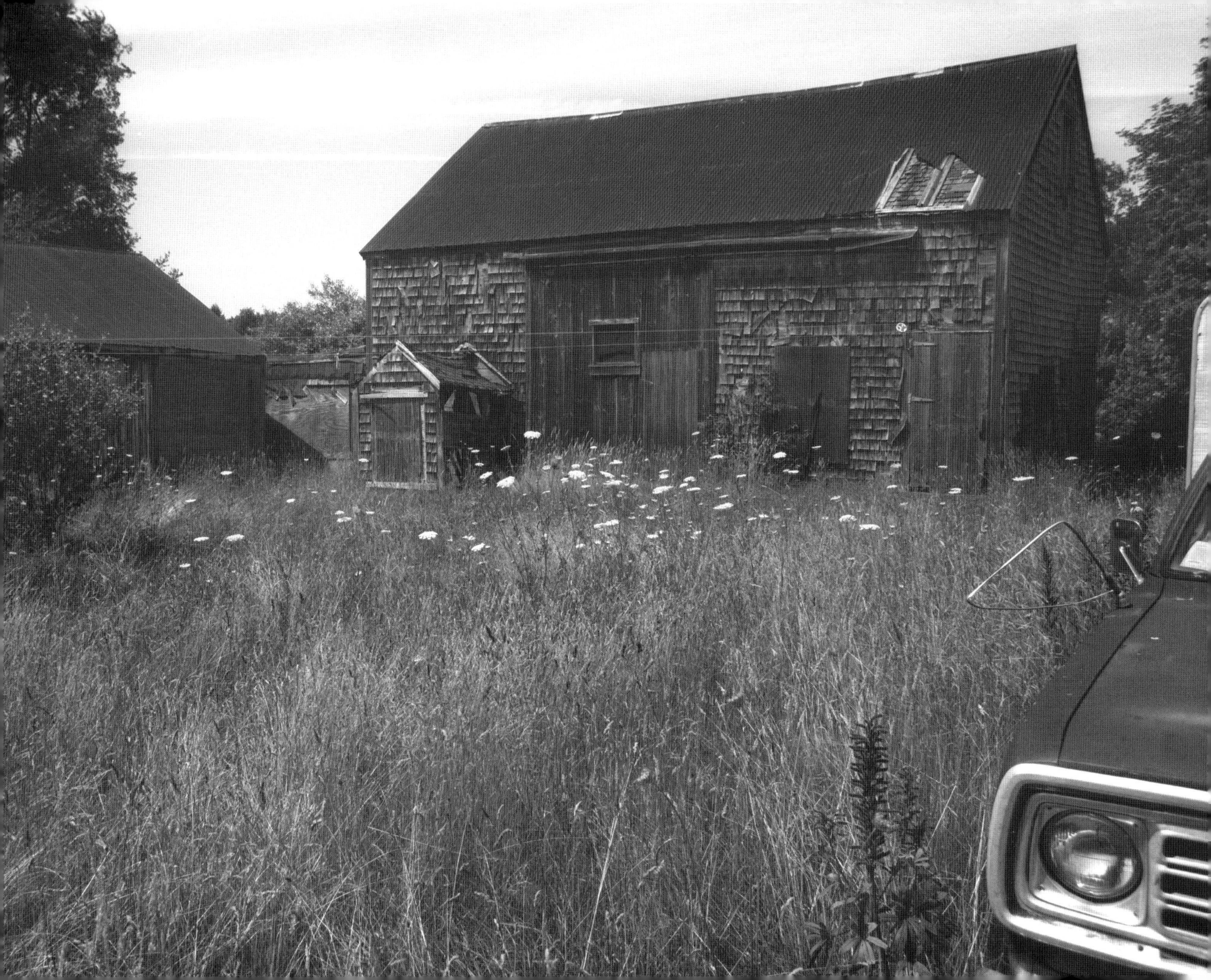

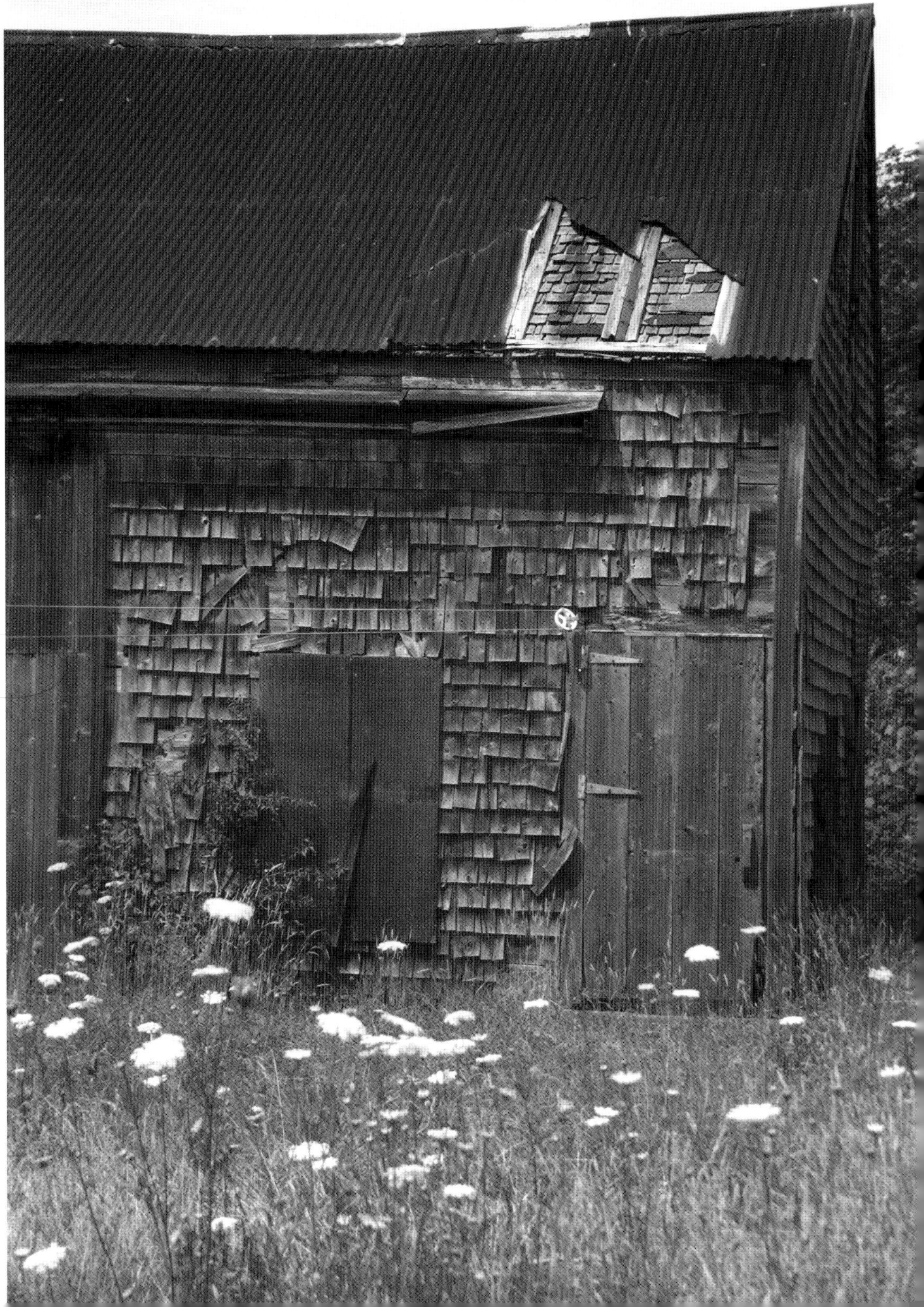

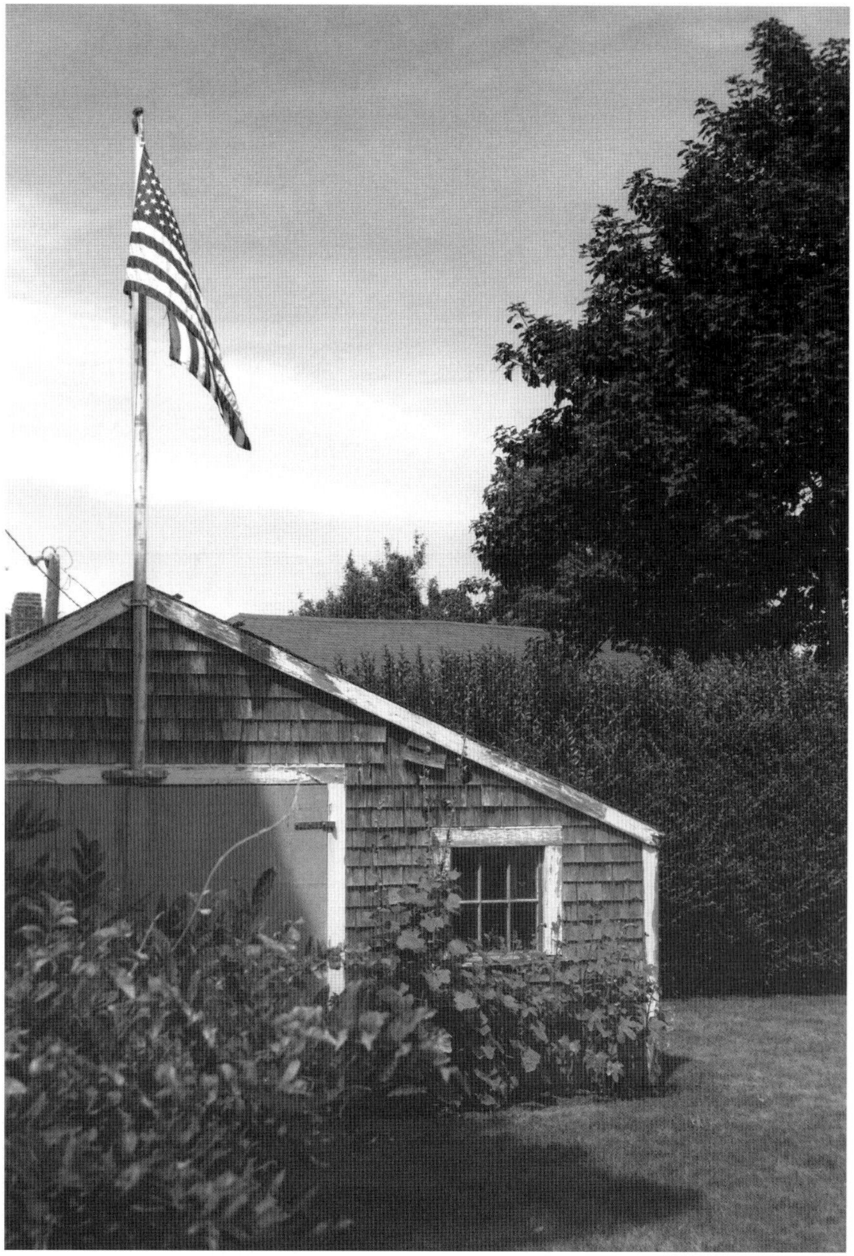

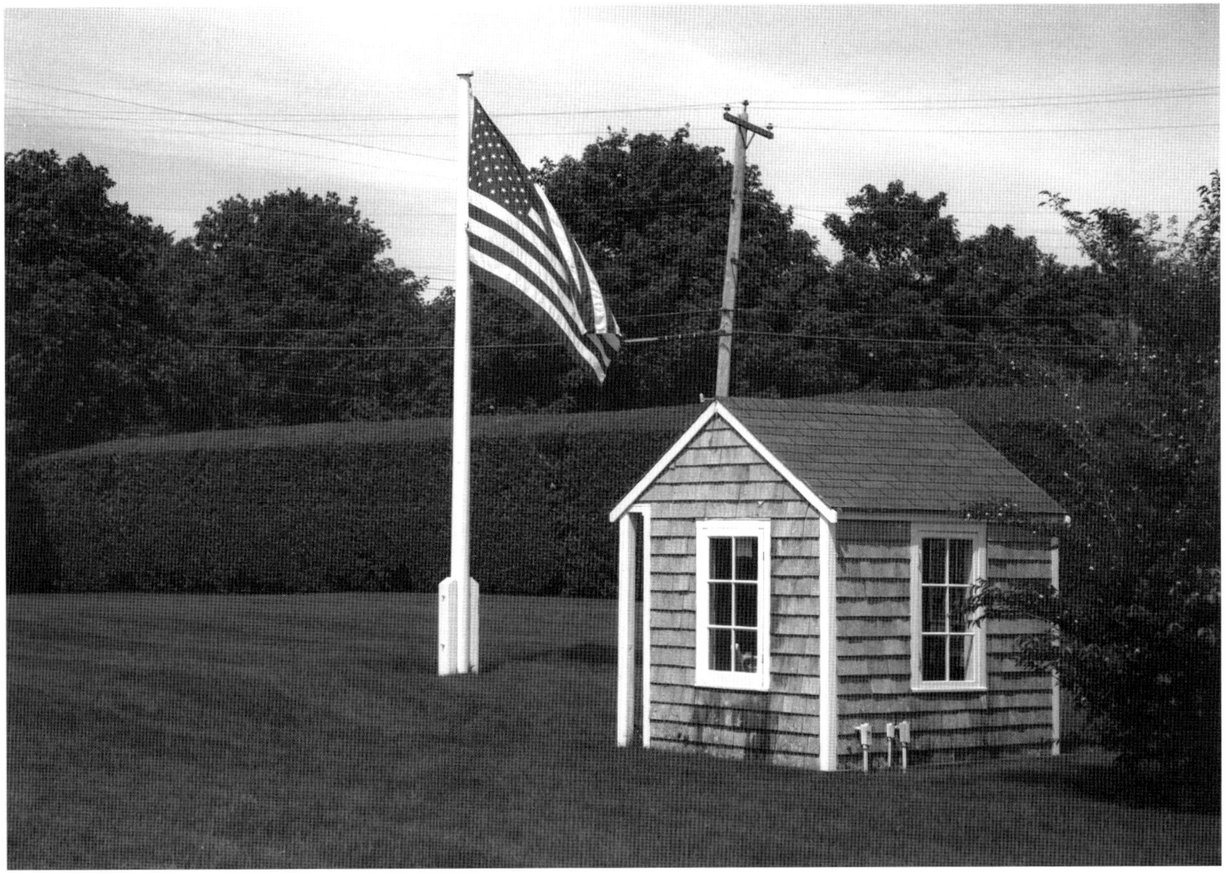

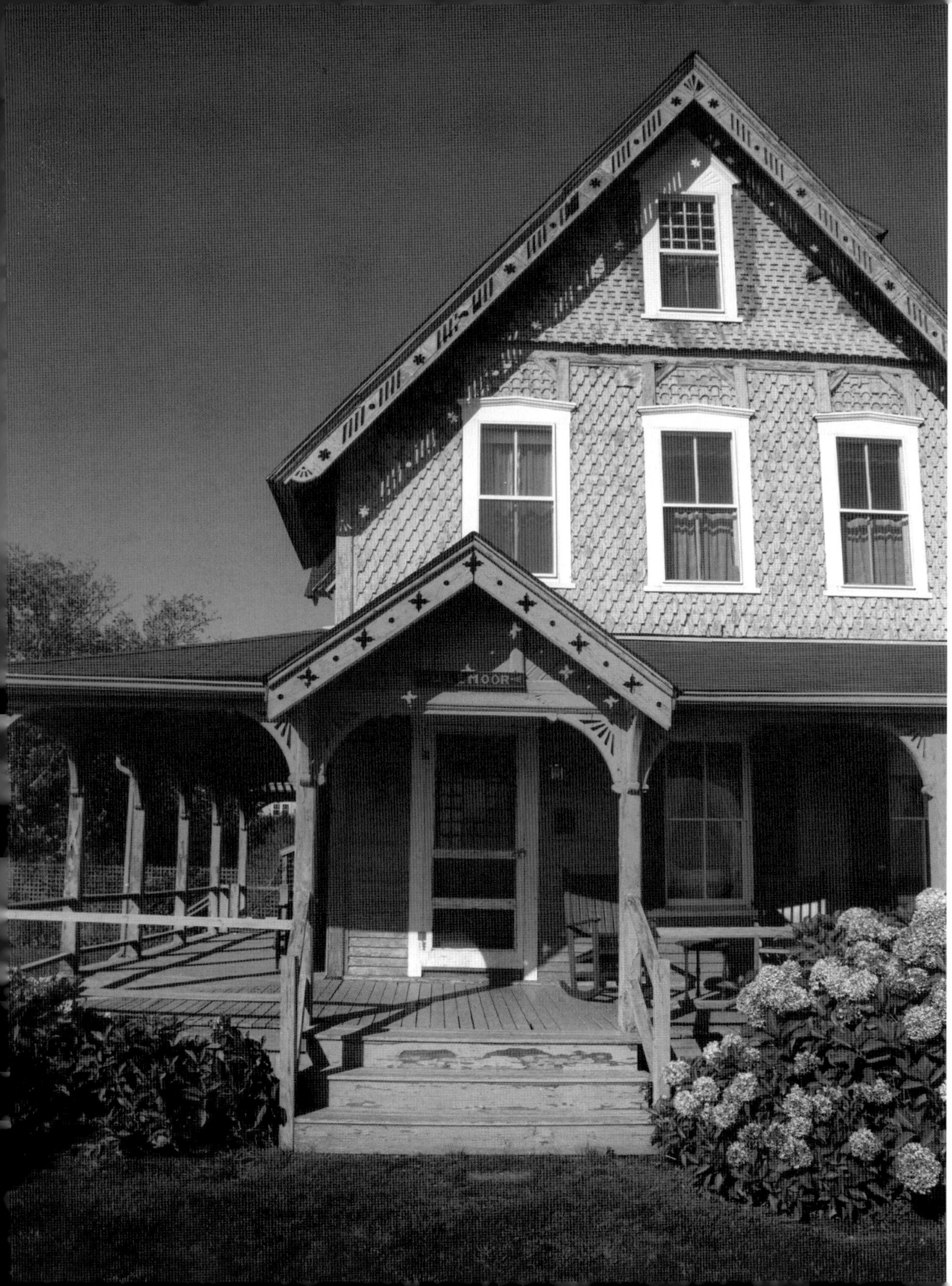
MOOR

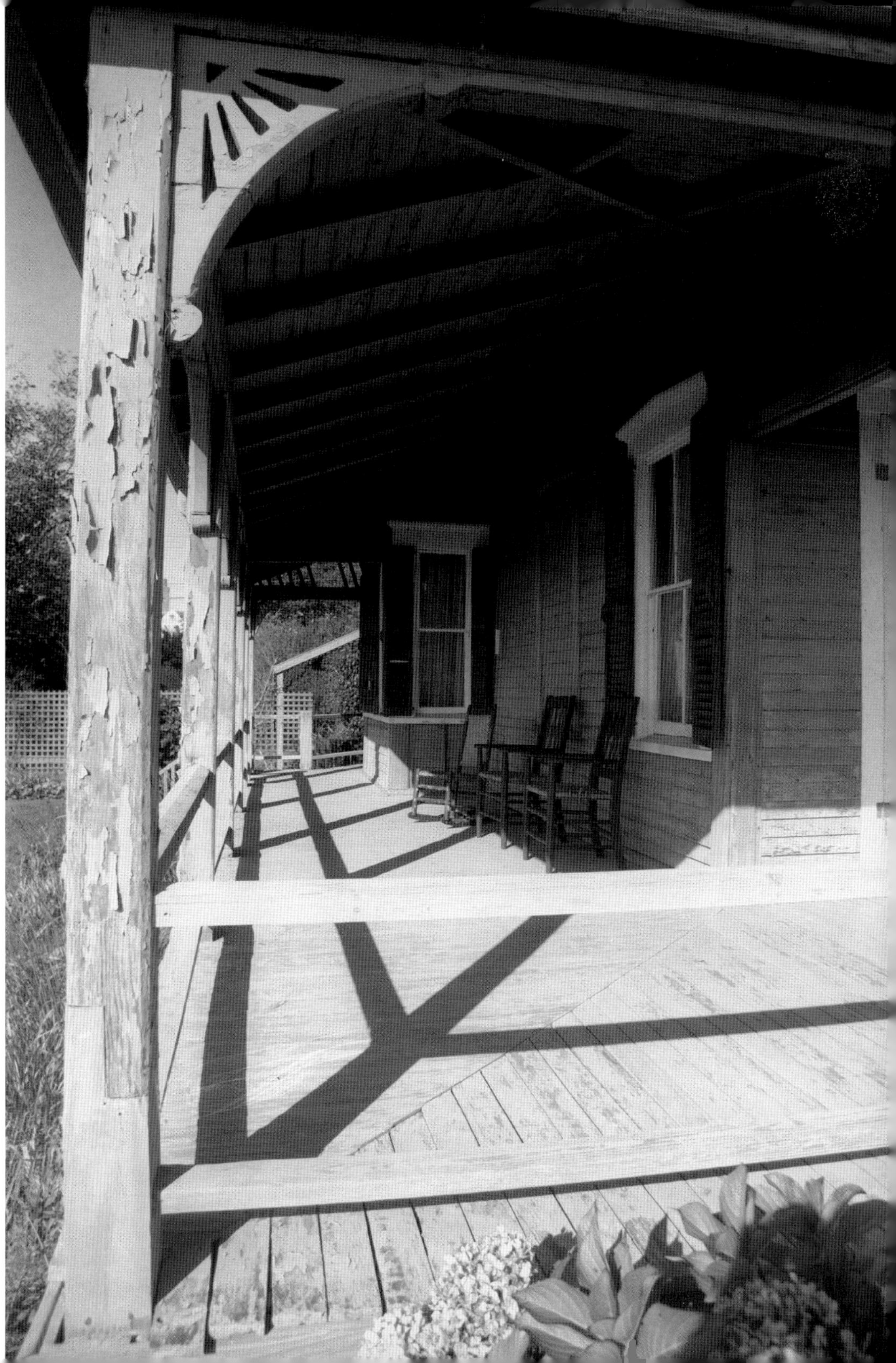

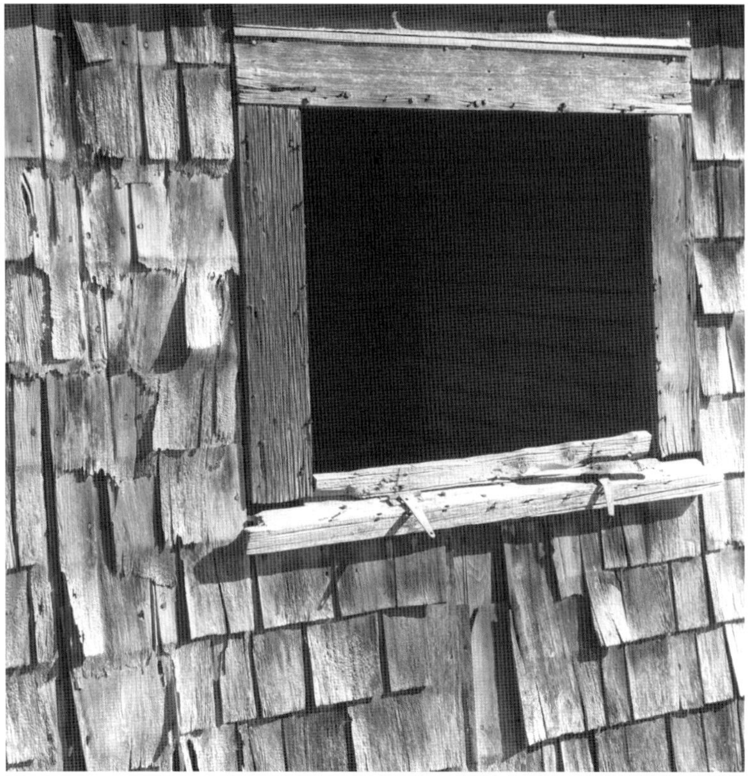

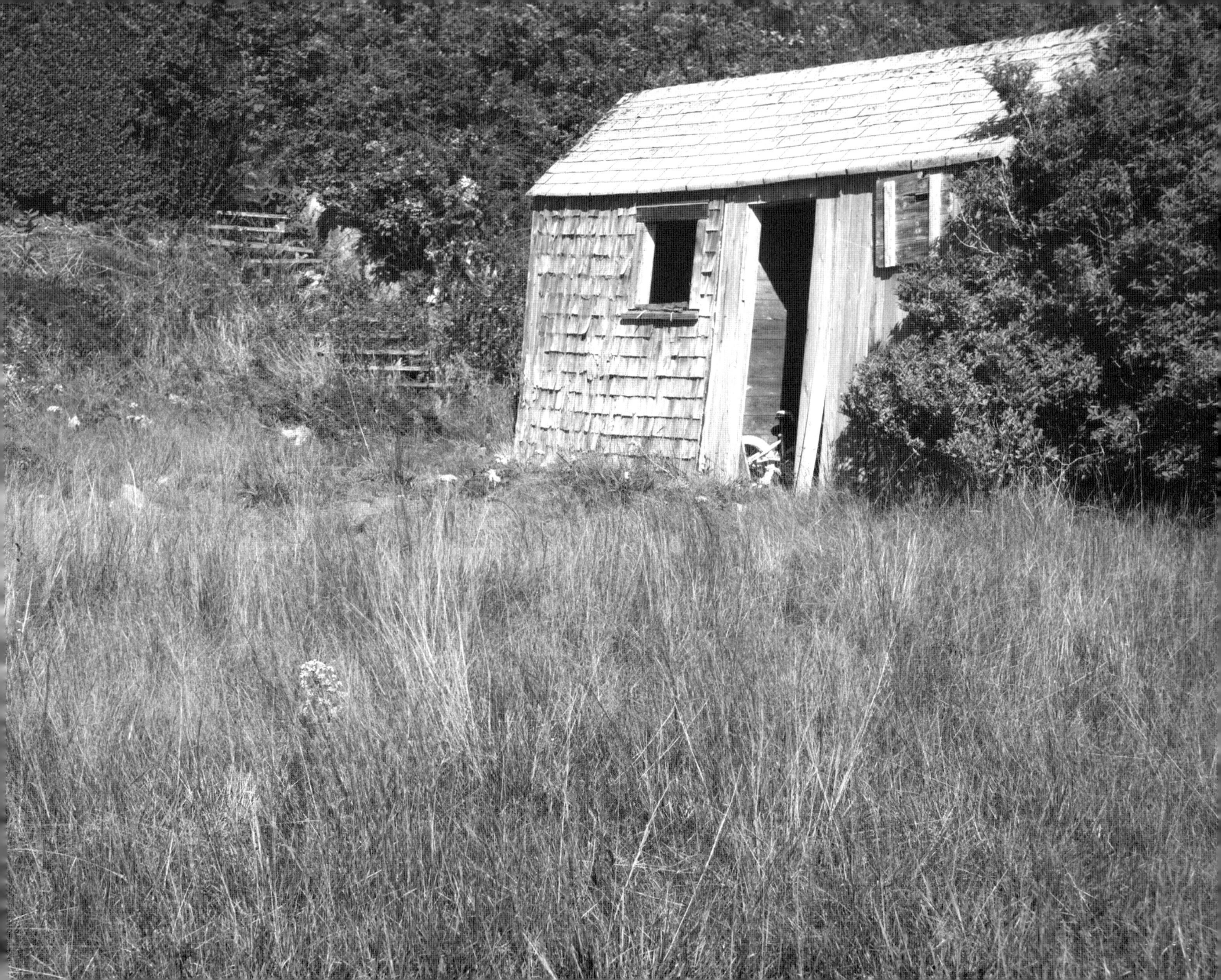

EPILOGUE

THOSE TAKEN BY NATURE

THOSE RESTORED BY MAN

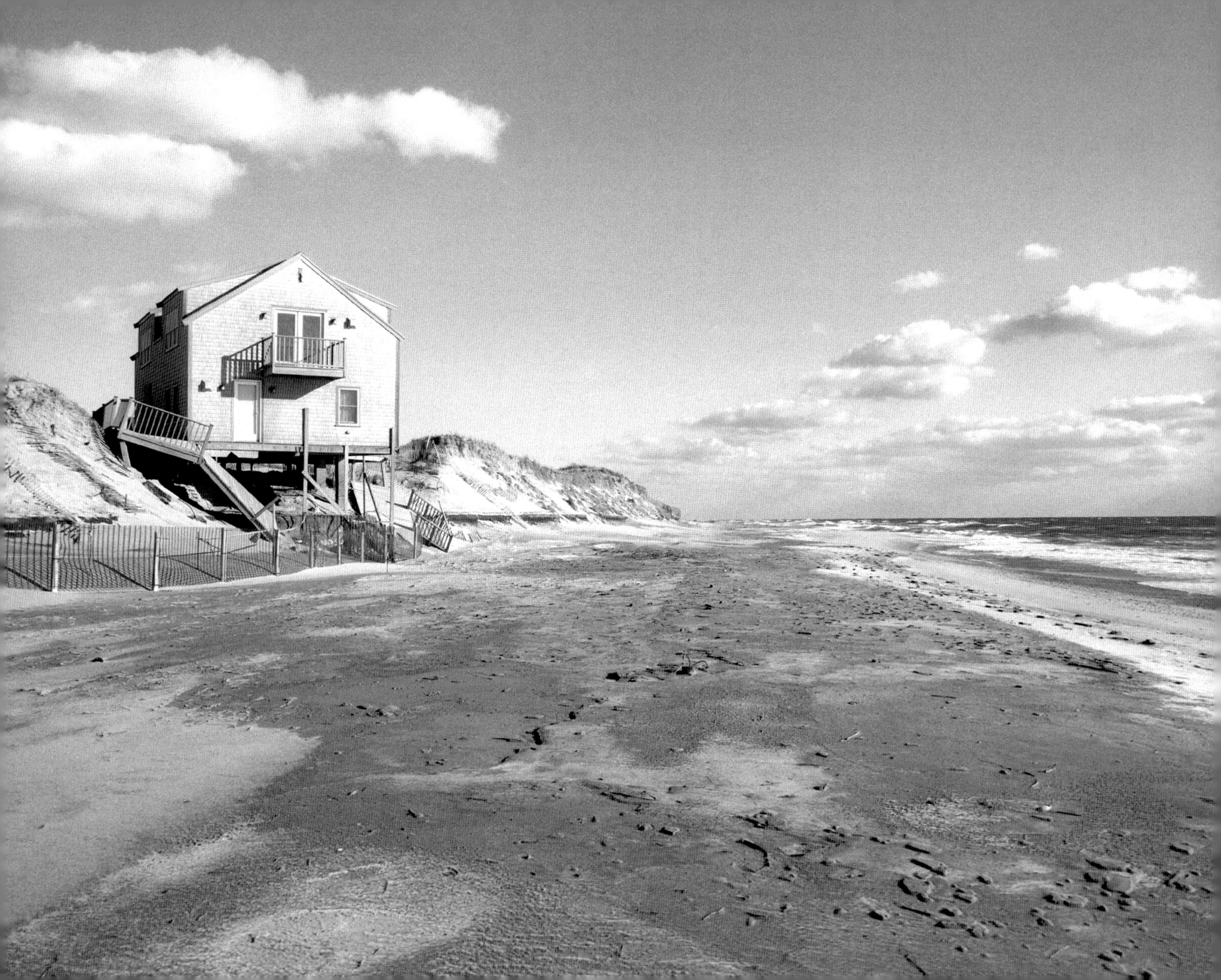

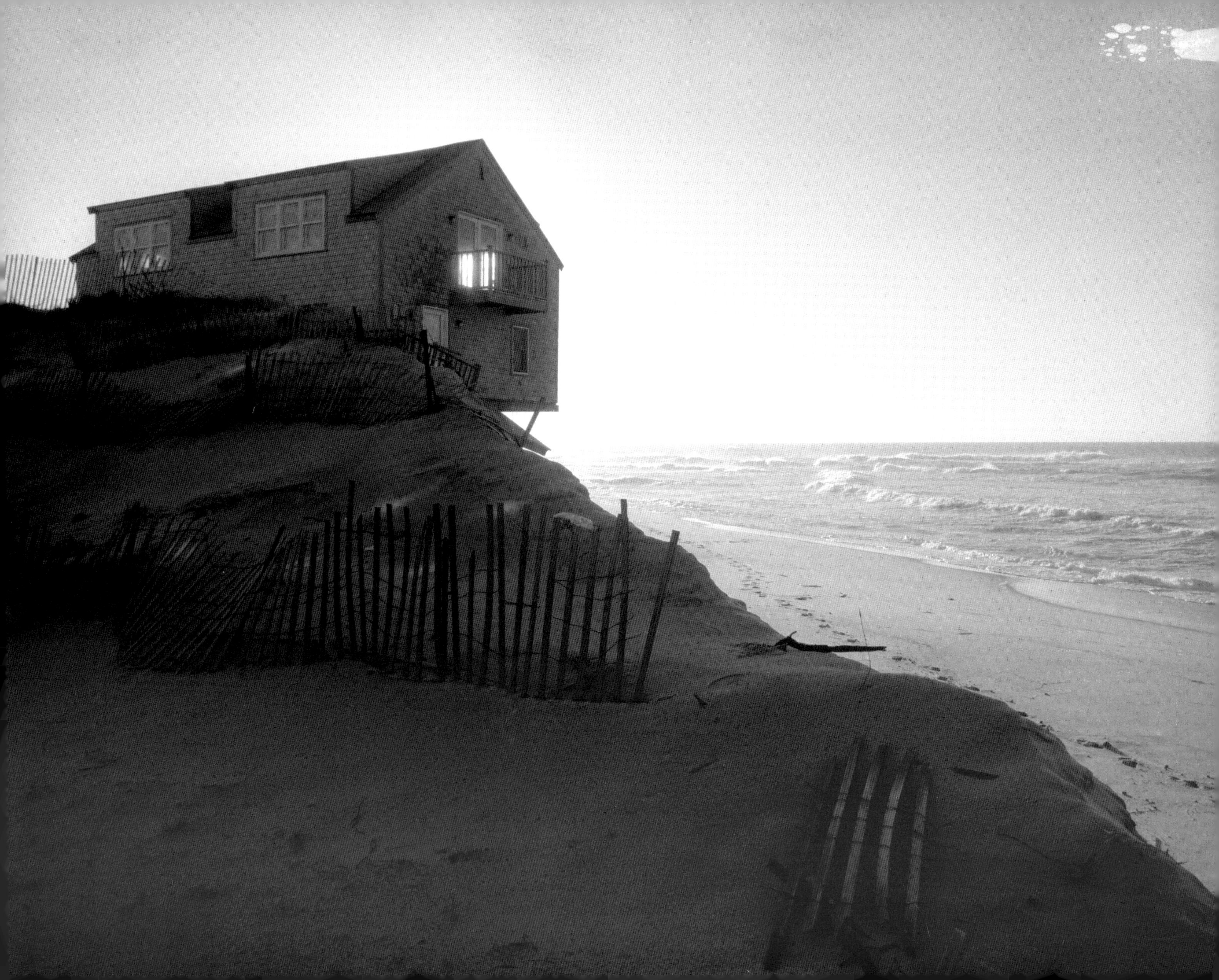

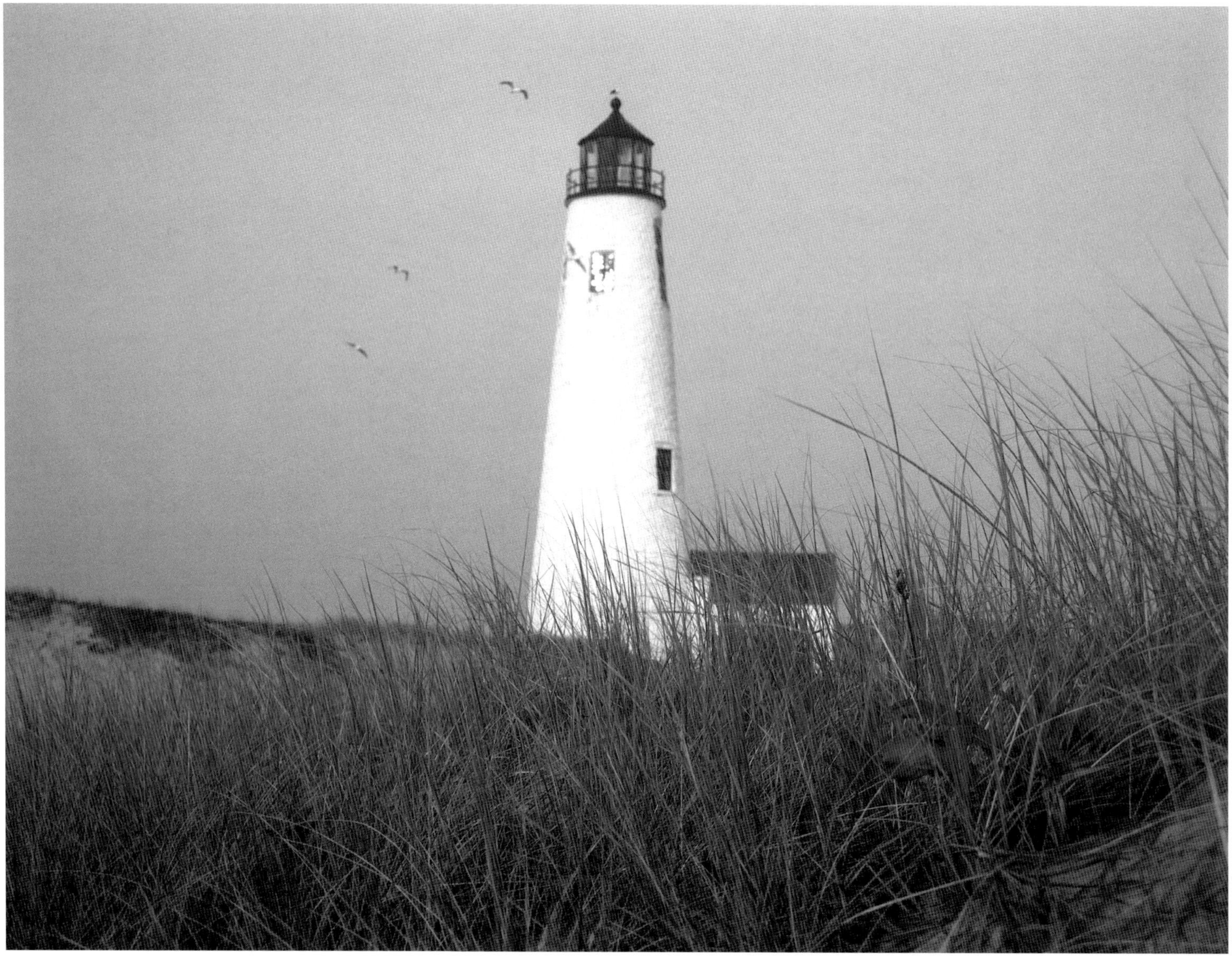

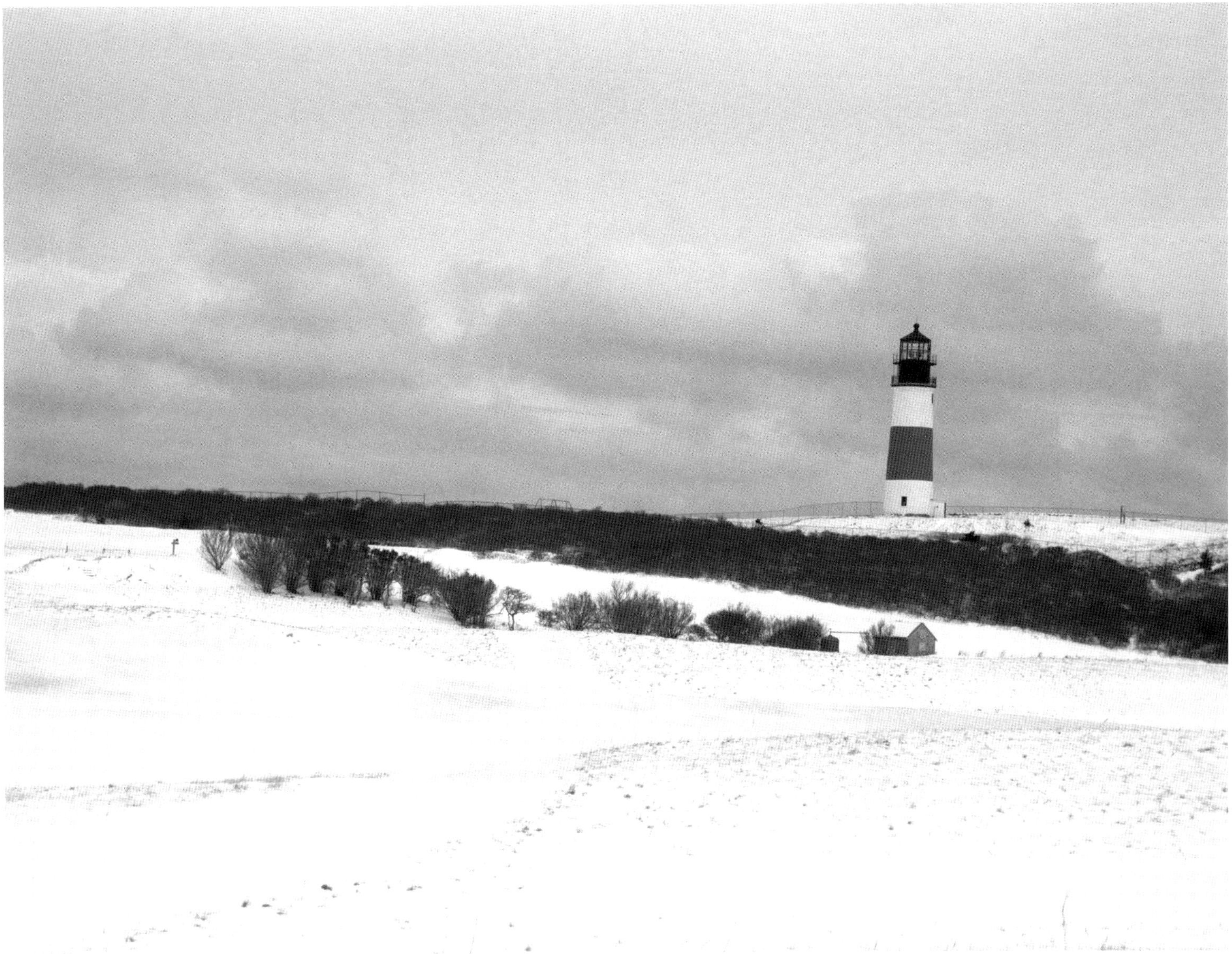

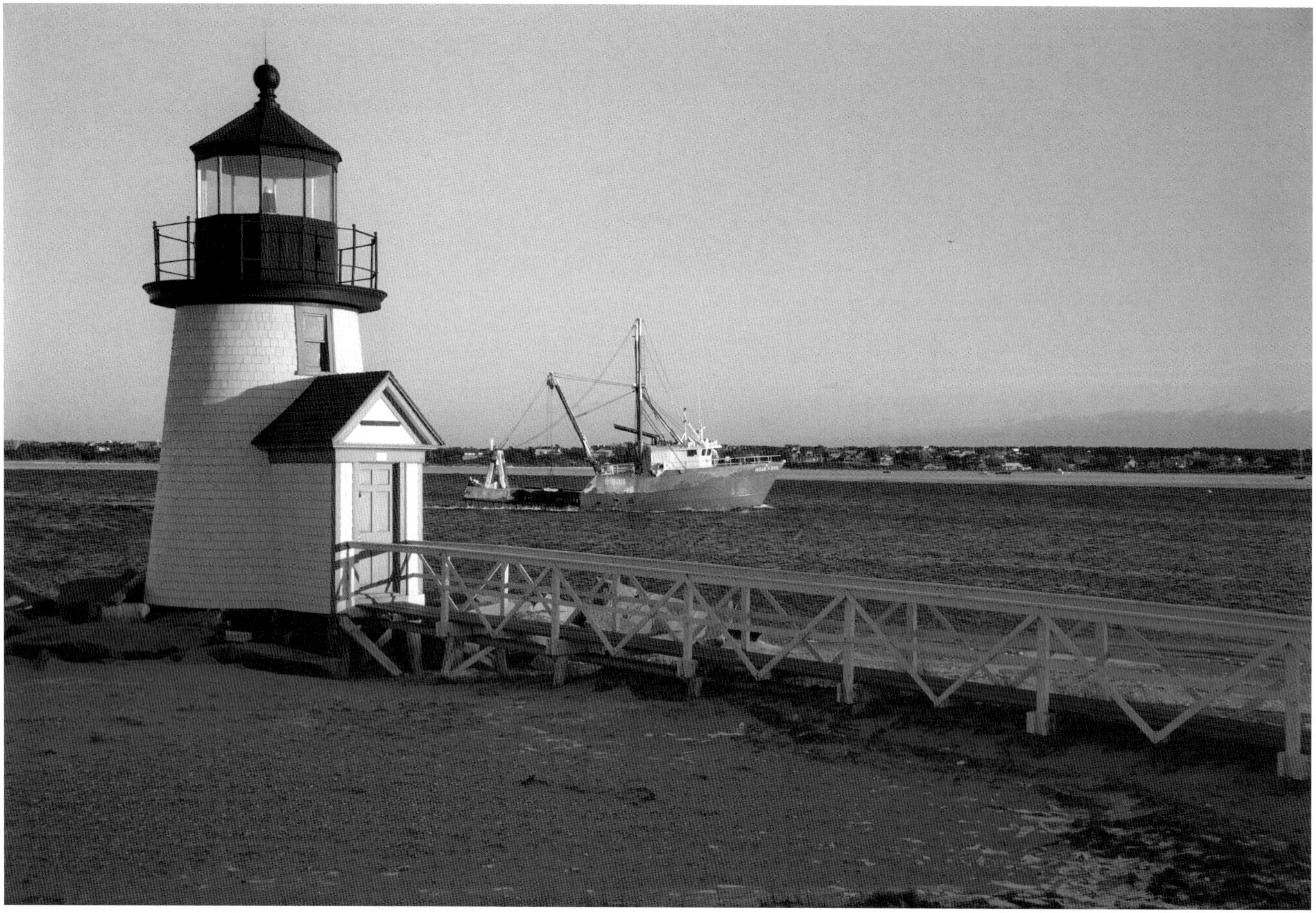

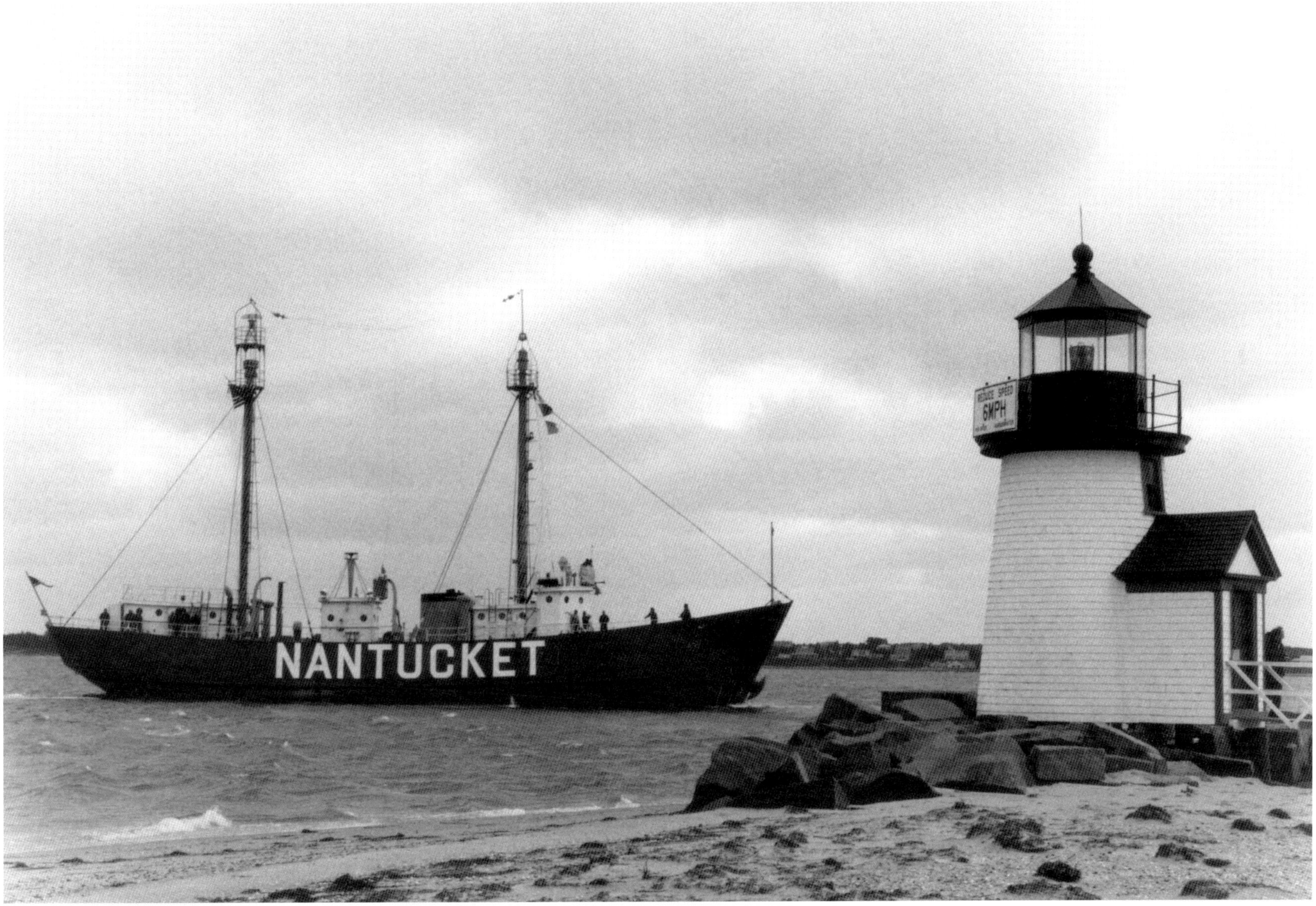
NANTUCKET
6MPH

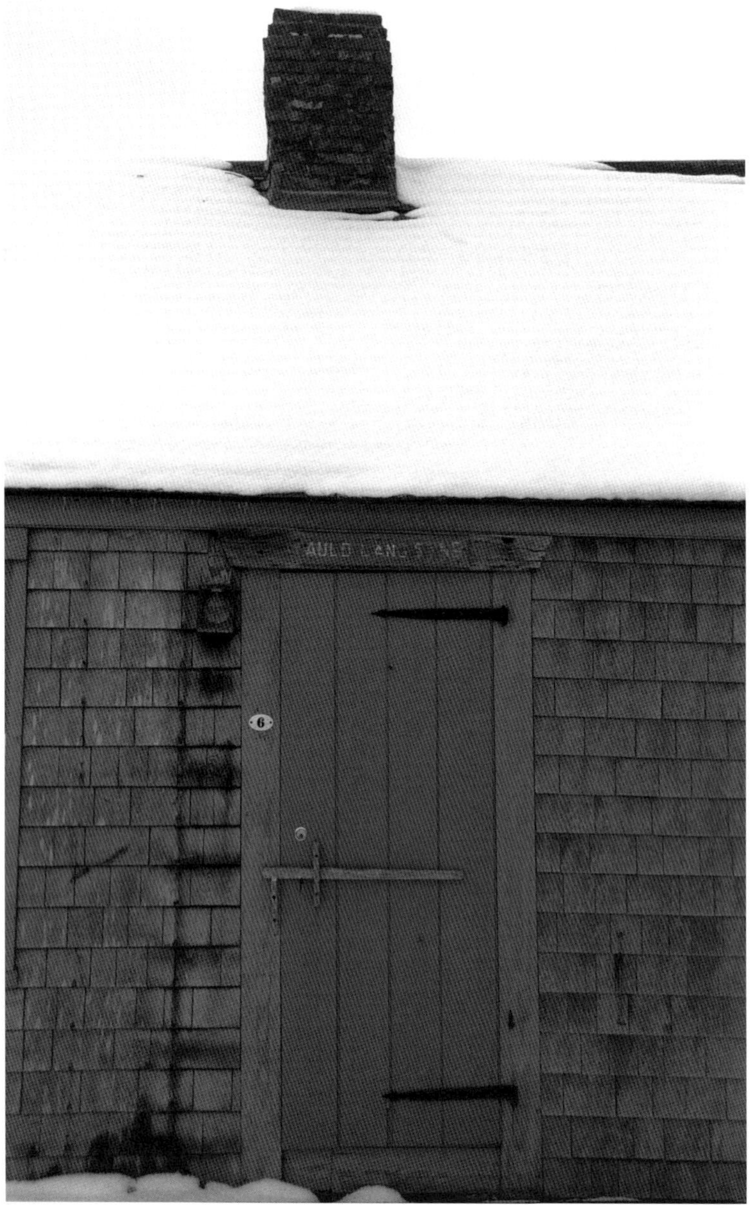
6

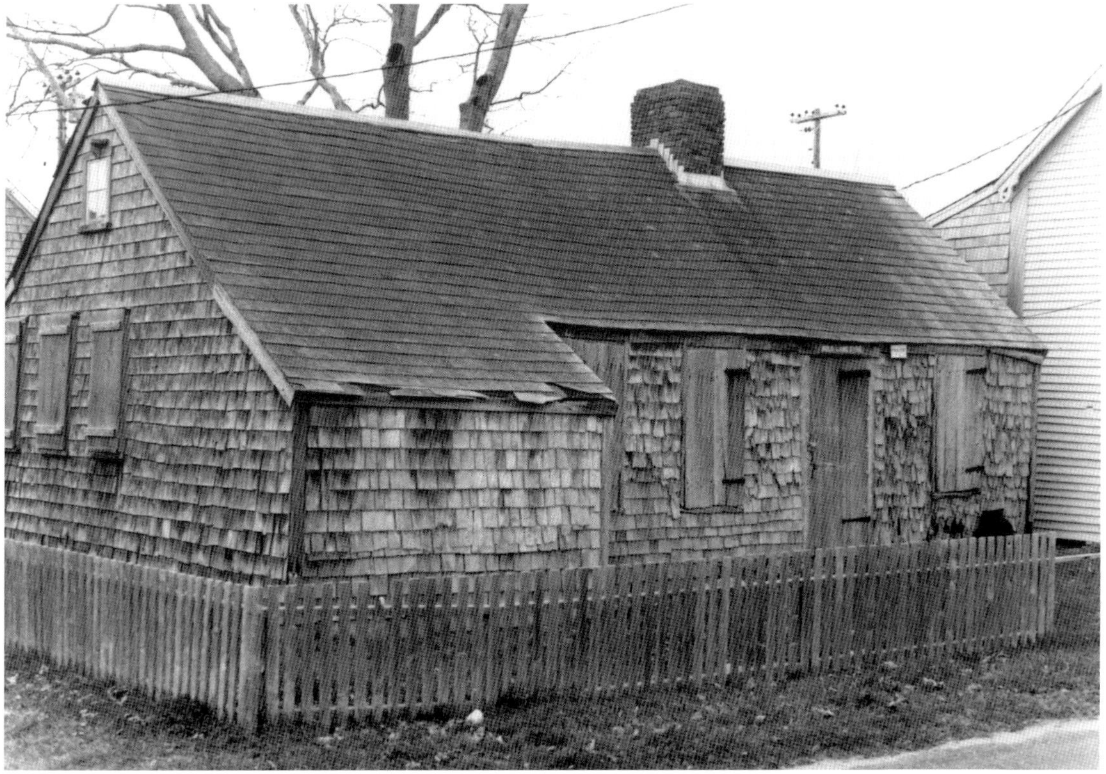

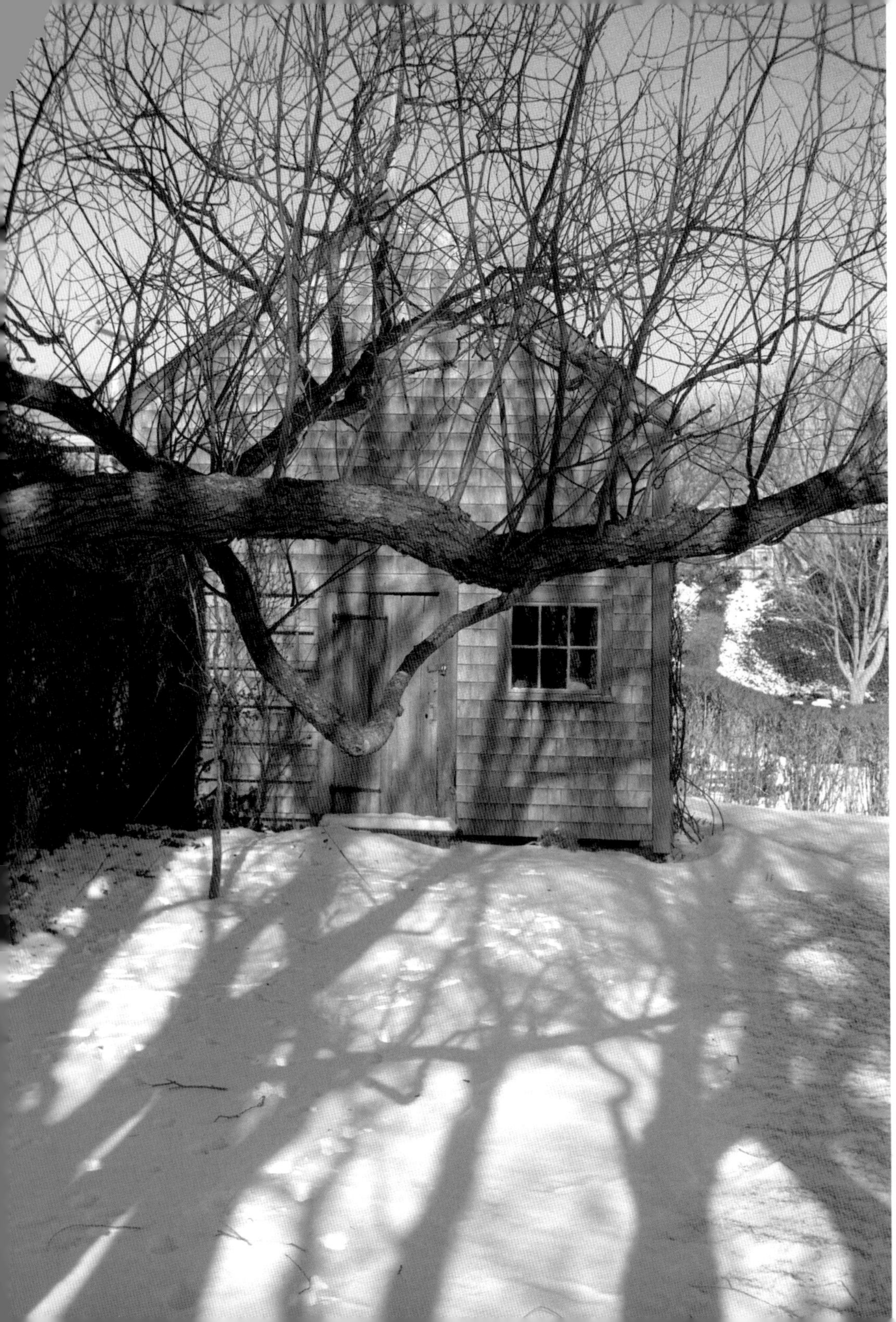

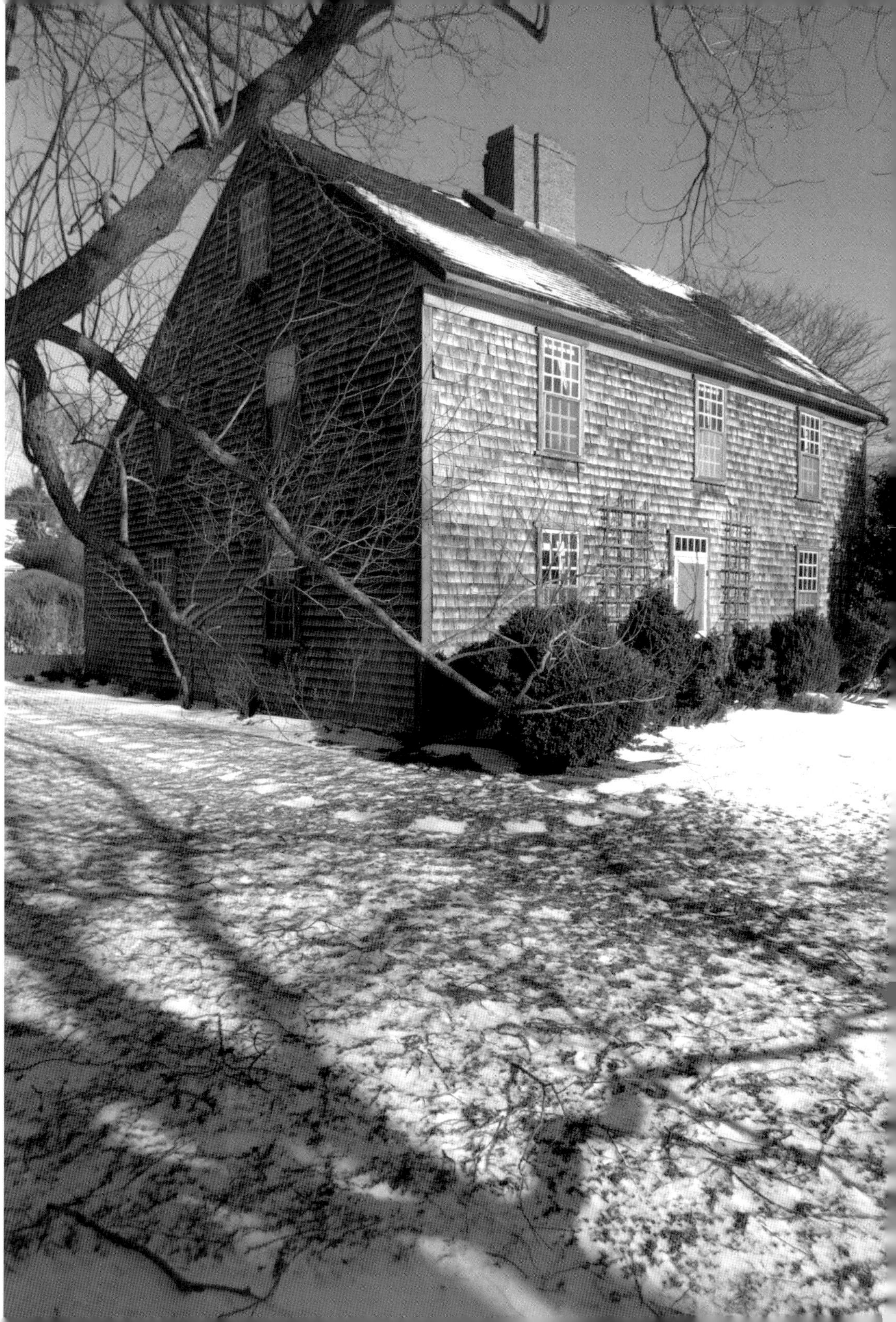

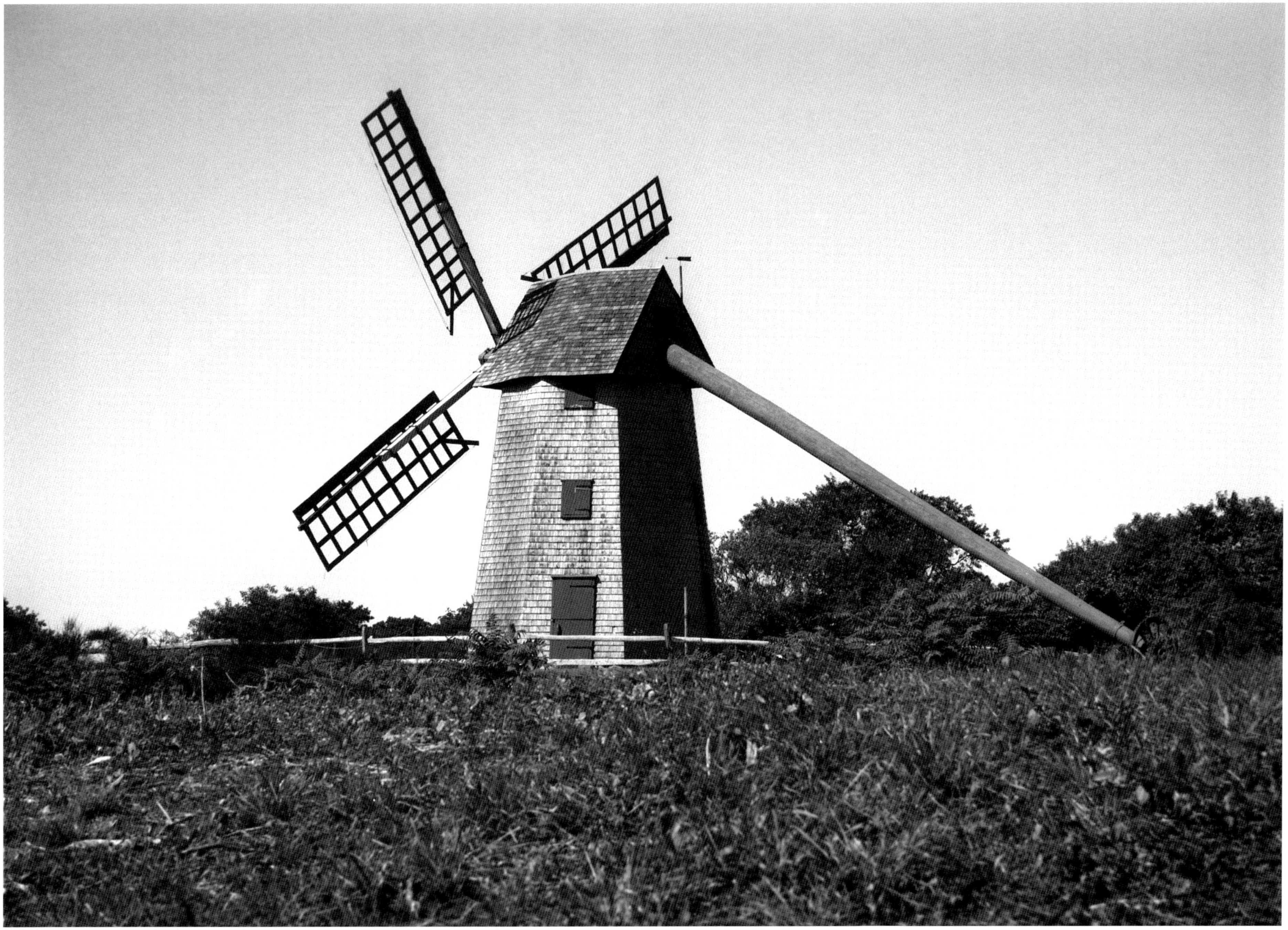

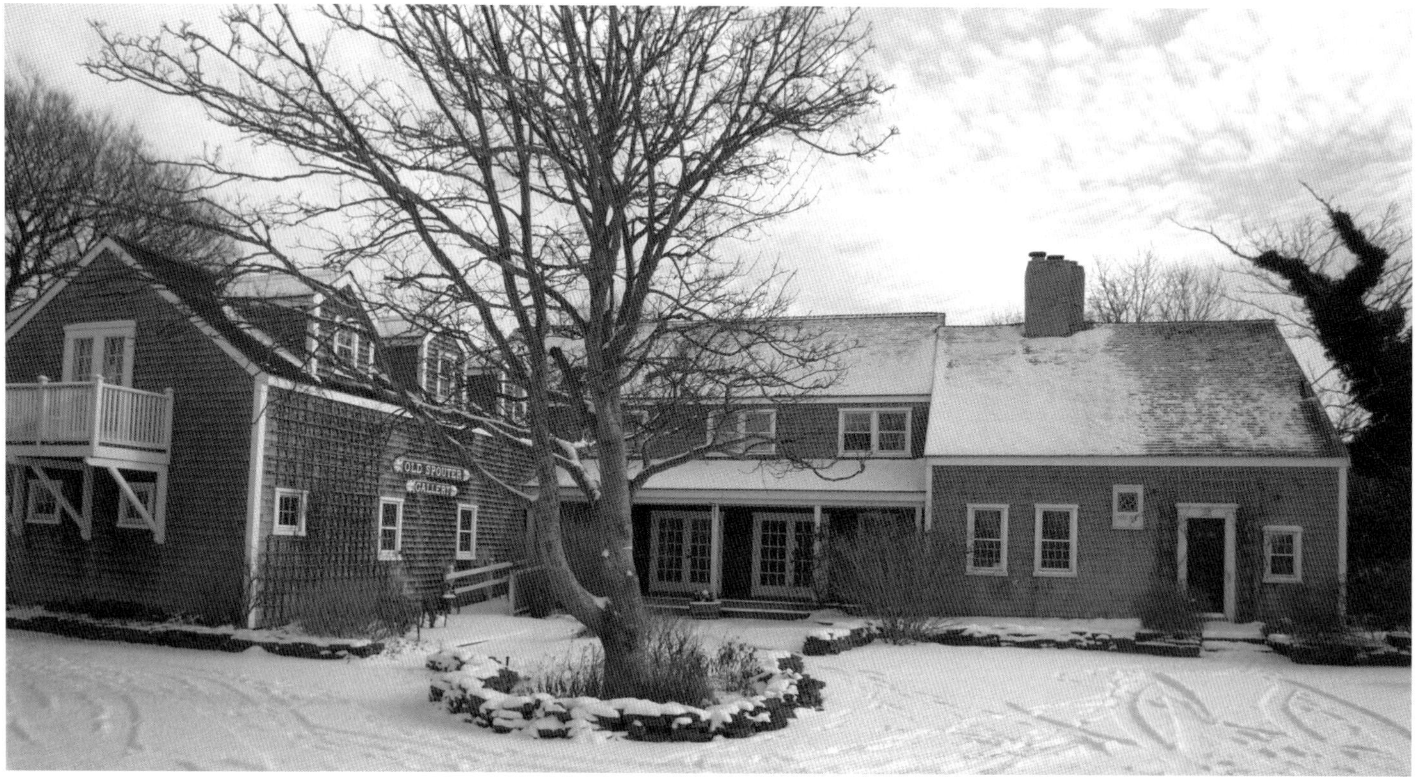

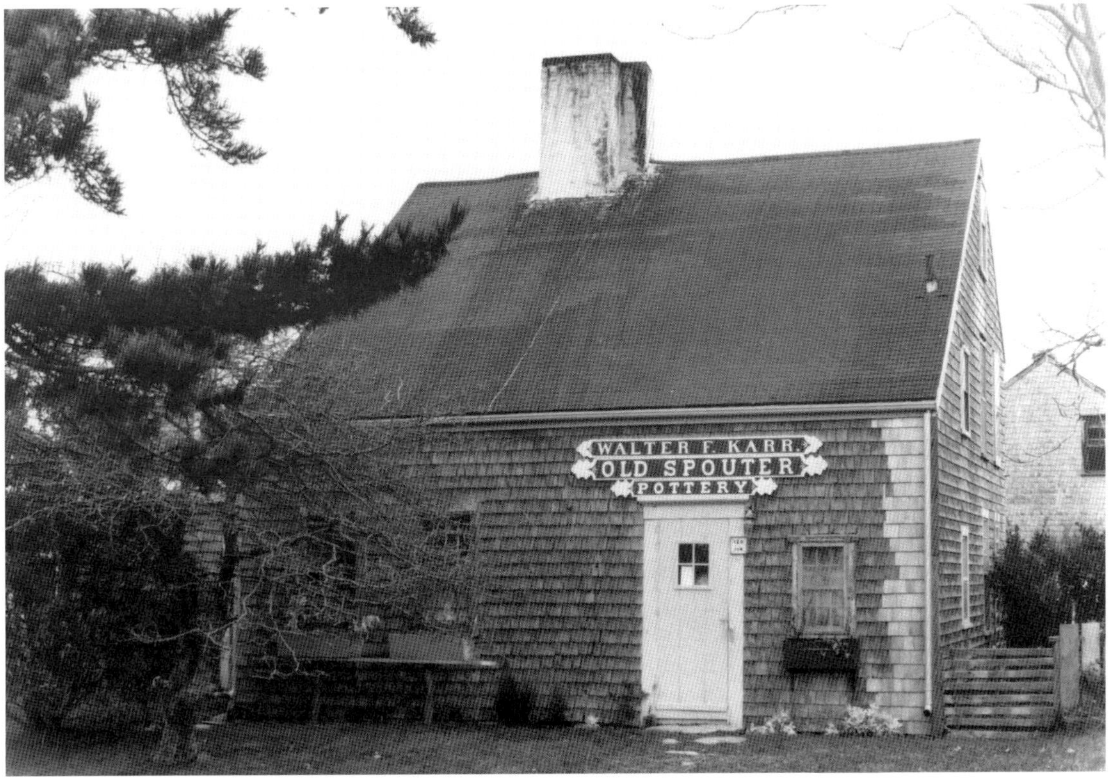
WALTER F. KARR
OLD SPOUTER
POTTERY

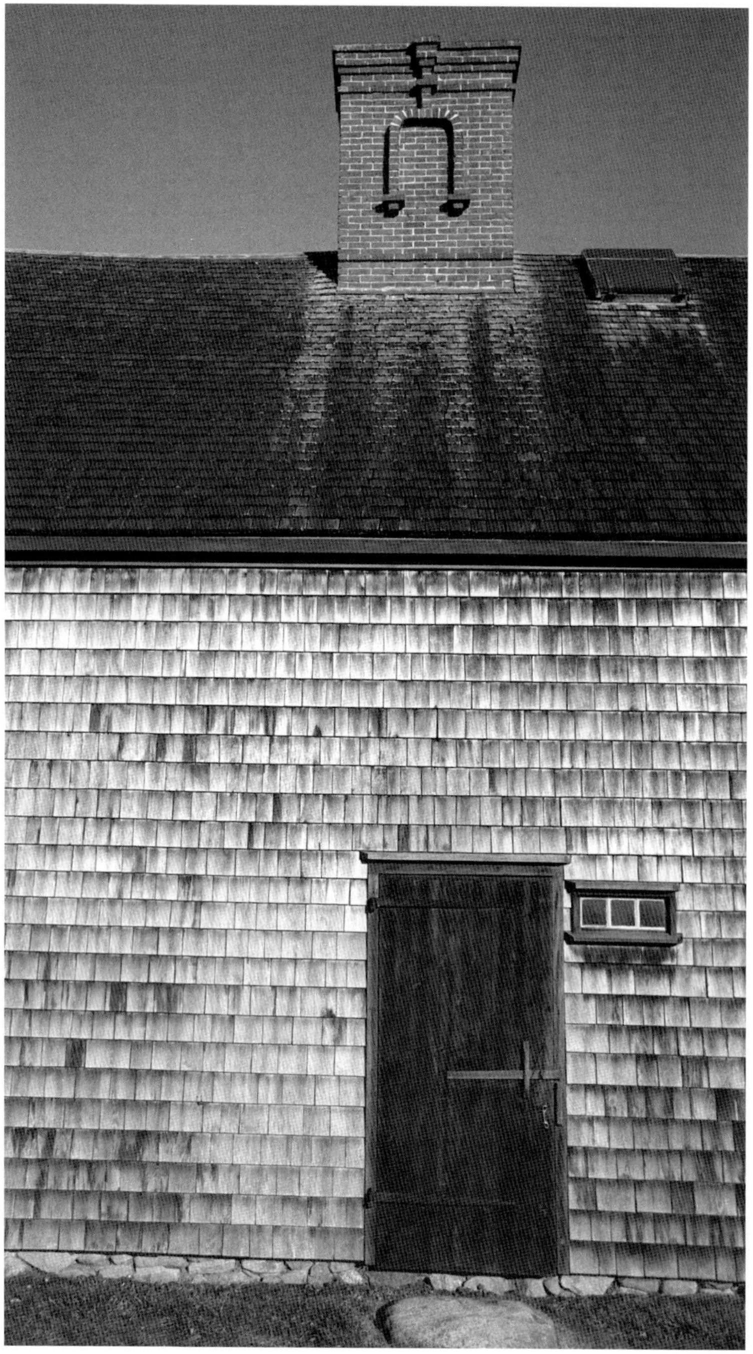

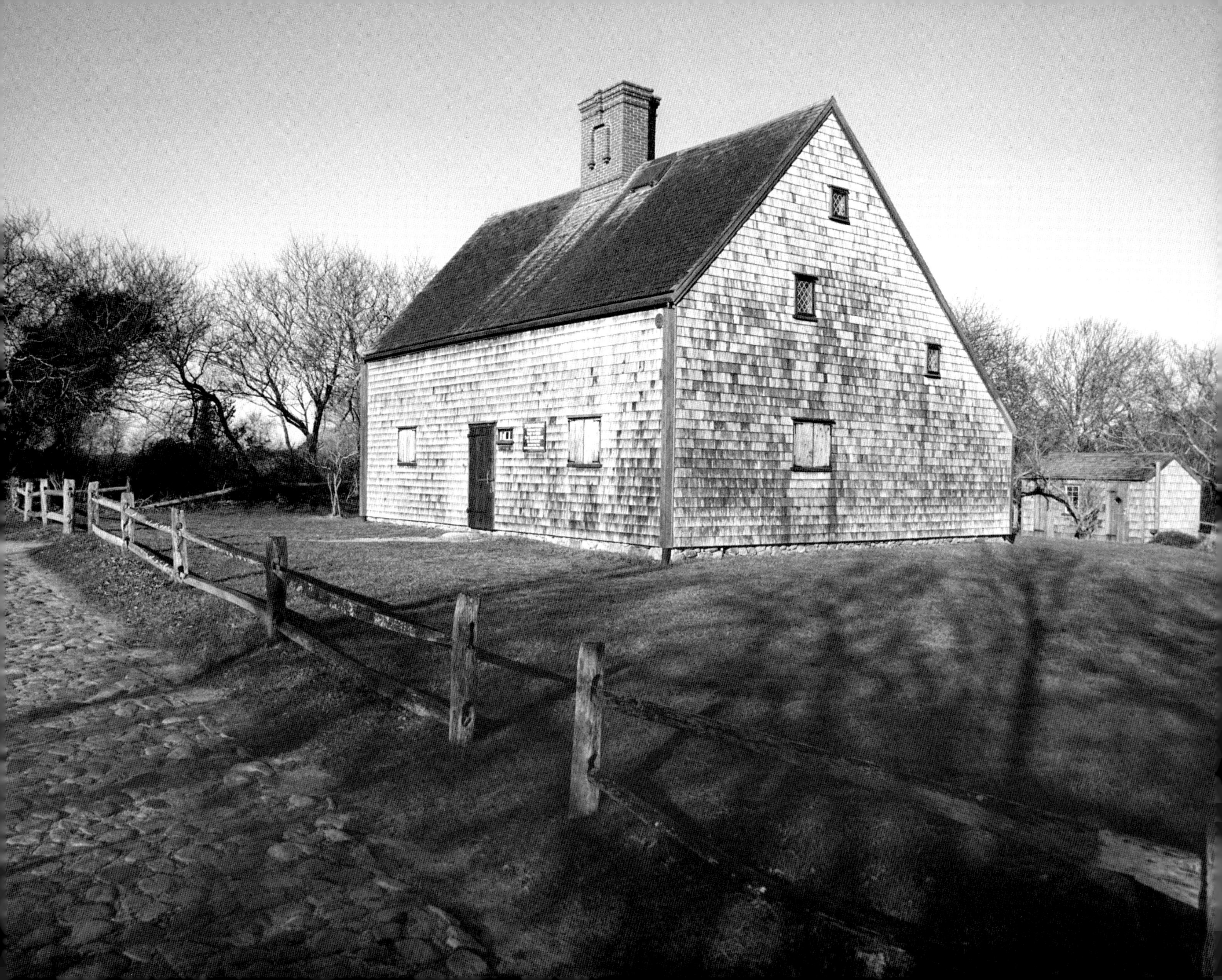

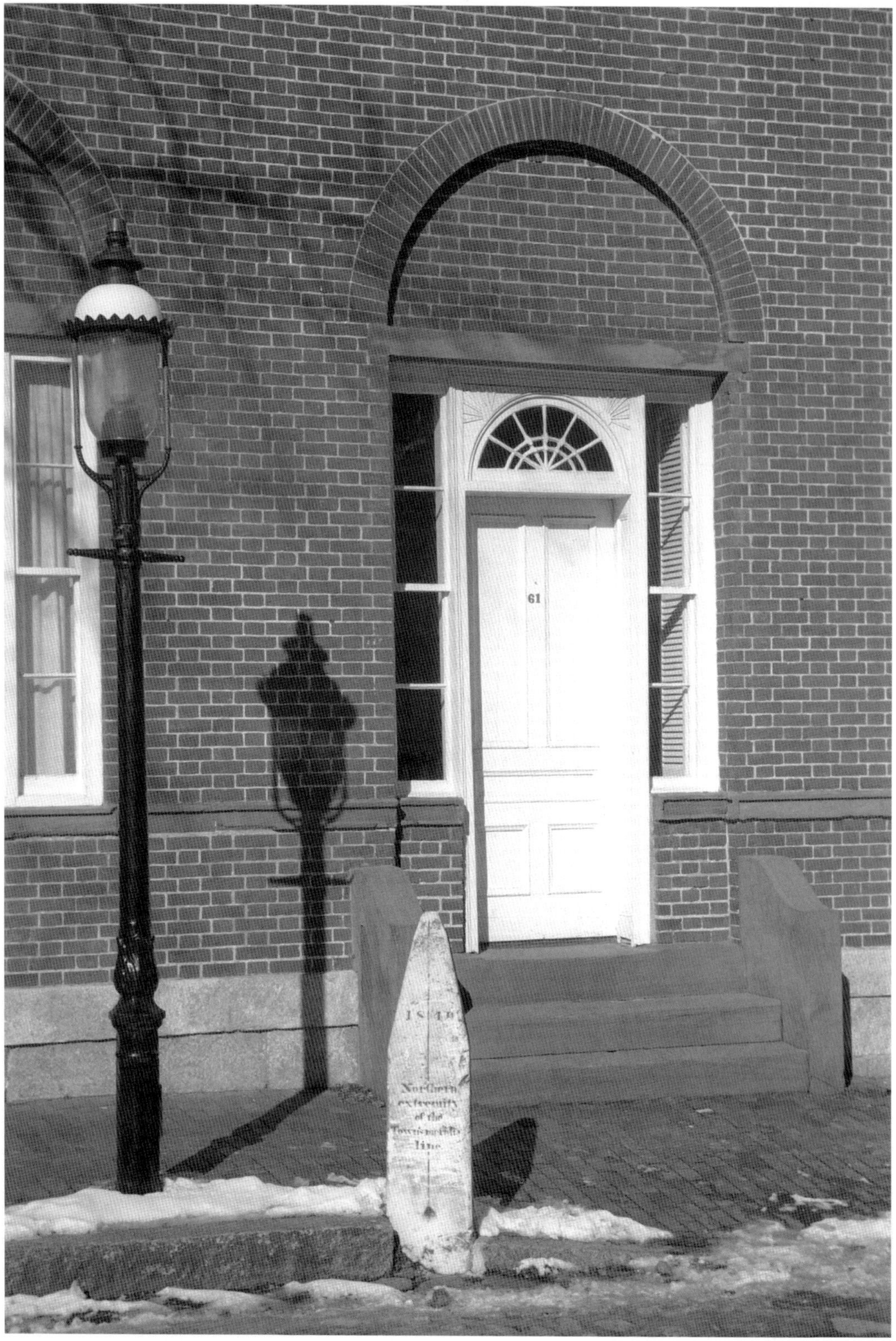
61
Northern
extremity
of the
line

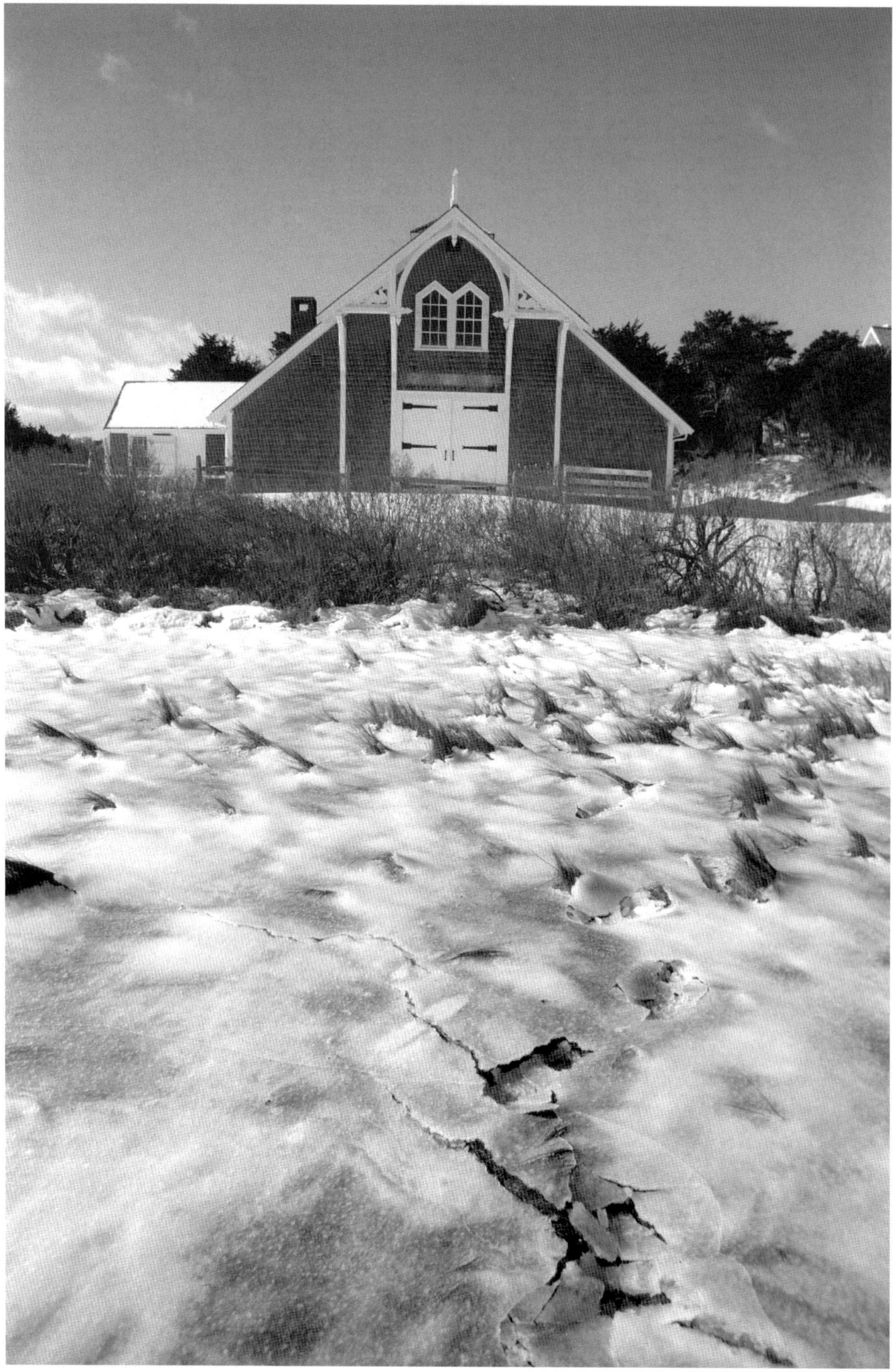

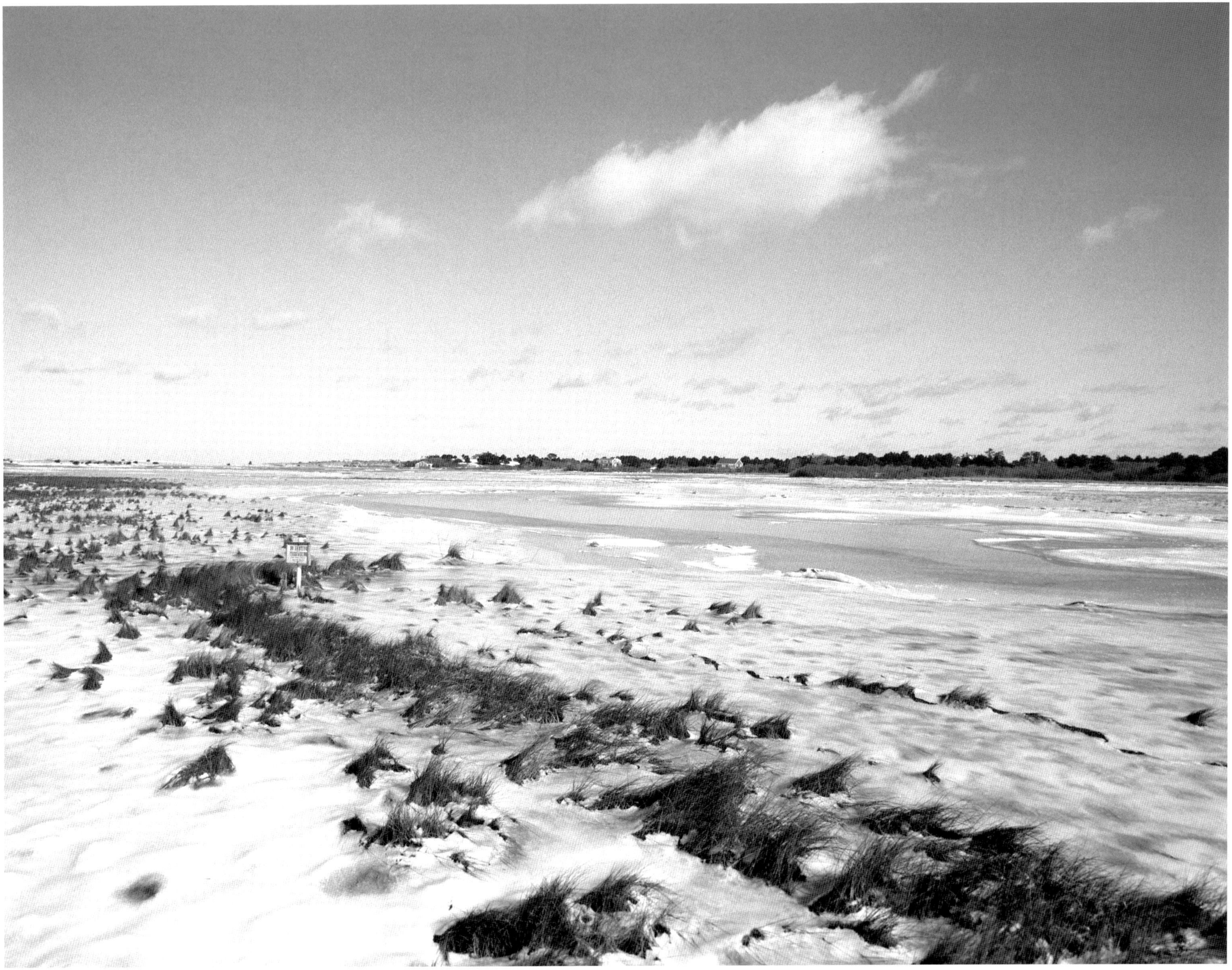

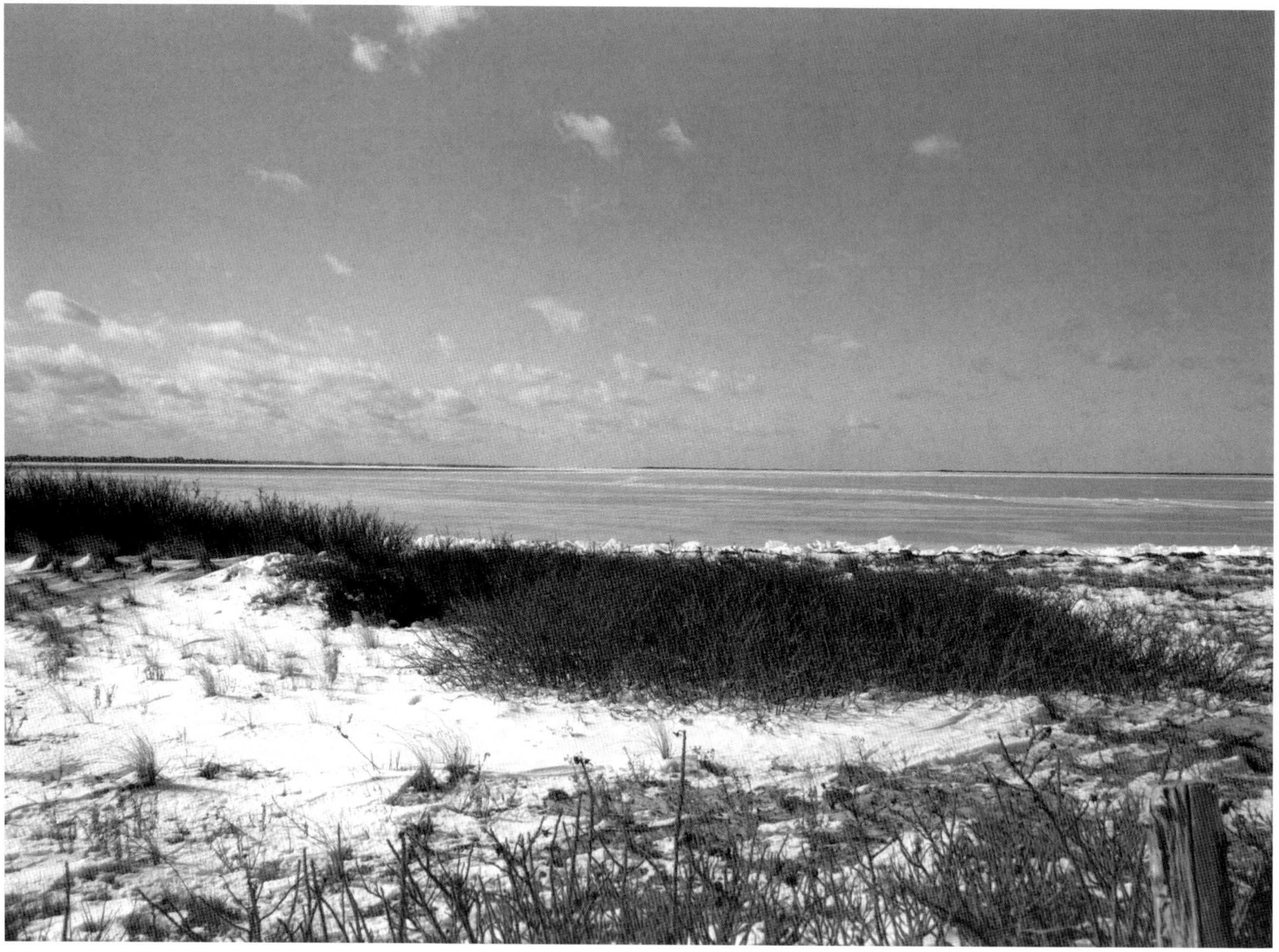

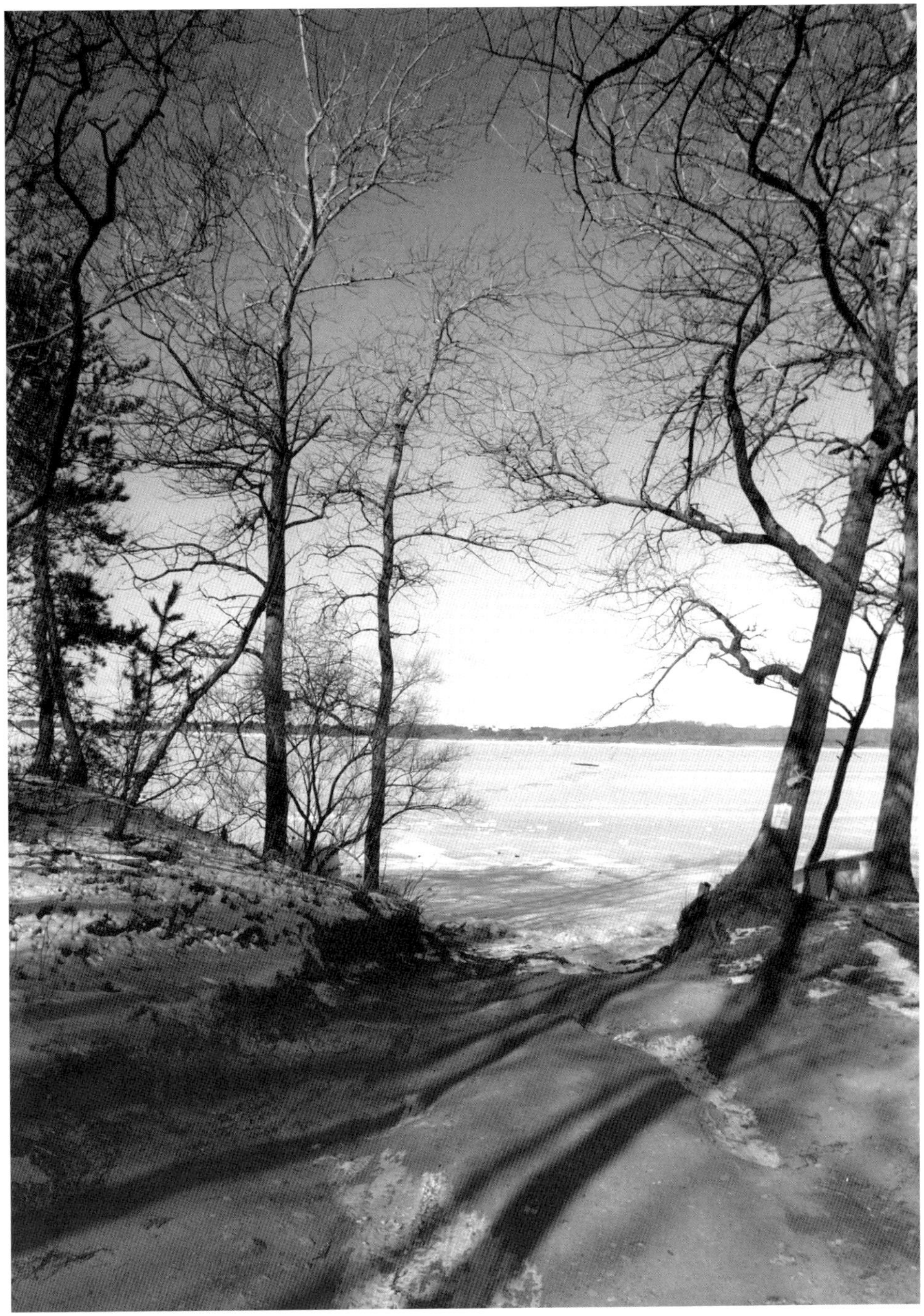

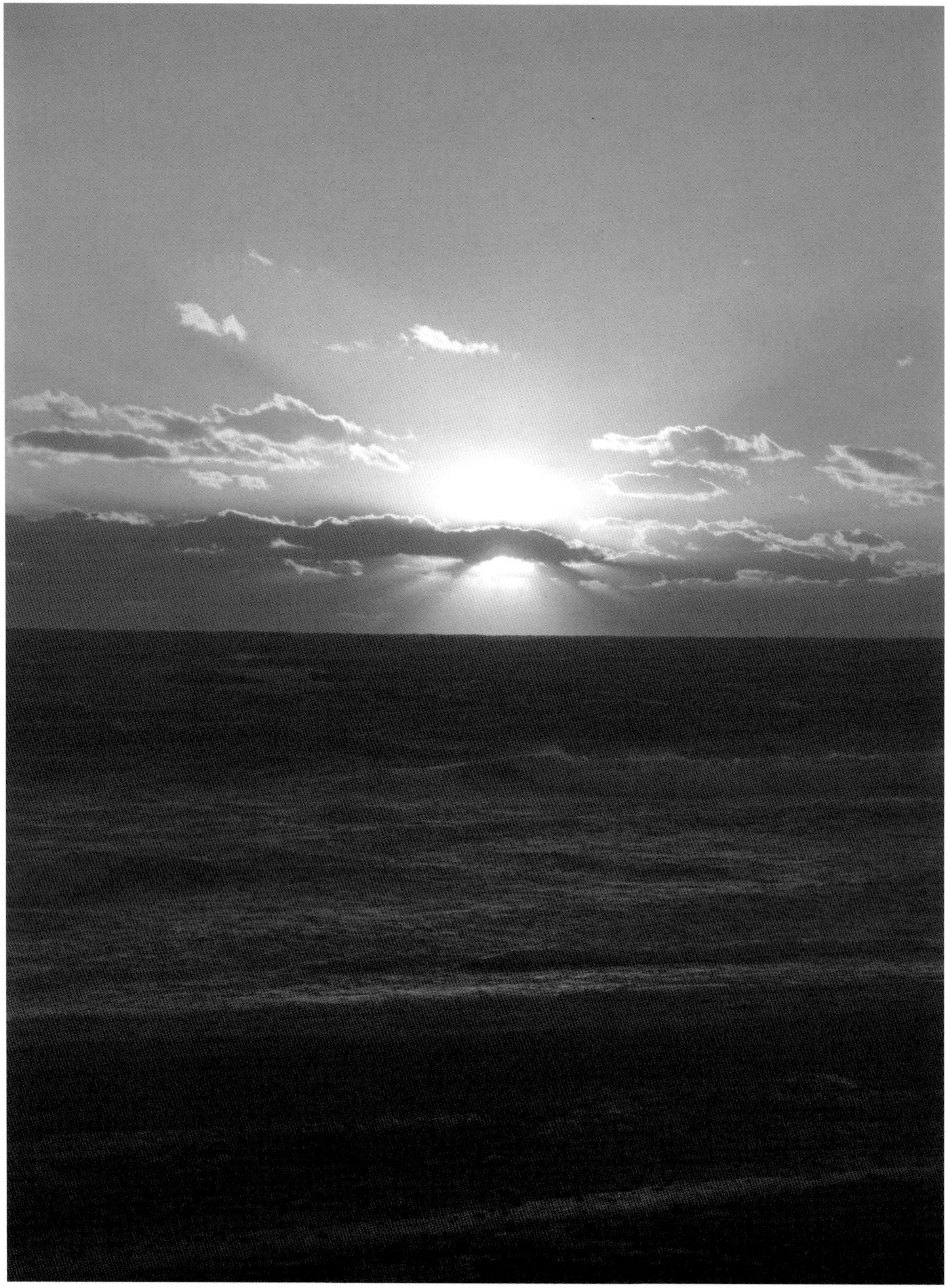

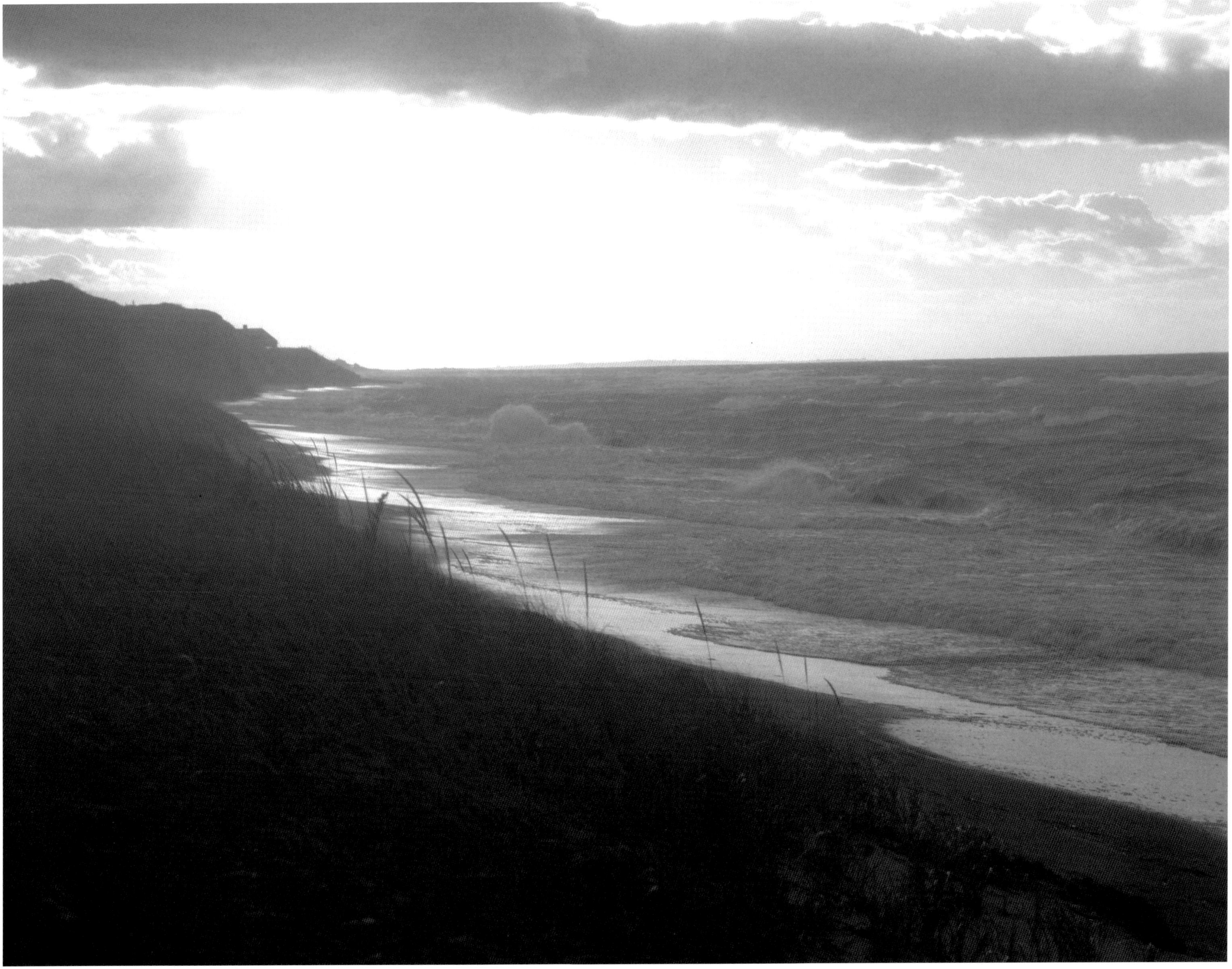

INDEX

1 Sconset Sunrise **1-1-2000**
2, 3, 7 Old Lifesaving Station, Muskeget 1882
4, 5, 6 Fishing Shack, Muskeget
9 Old Lifesaving Station, Tuckernut
10 Beach Permits, Madaket
11 Thar She Goes, Madaket
12, 13 Beach House, Madaket
14 Beach Steps, Dionas
15 Geodesic Domes, Dionas
16 Washing Pond
17 Top Hat, Dionas
18, 19 Reed Pond
20, 21 Dionas Cottage
22, 23 Union Street
24, 25 Upper Orange Street
26, 27 Lower Orange Street
28, 29 Upper Main Street
30, 31 Civil War Monument Circle

32 Old School House, Pleasant Street
33 Shed, York Street
34 Kitchen, Gardner Street
35 Kitchen, Howard Court
36 Shed, Howard Street
37 Main Street
38, 39 Brant Point 1746
40, 41 Old North Wharf
42, 43 Sheds, Lower Orange
44 Creeks
45 Creeks Cottage
46, 47 Milestone Road Barn
48, 49 Ram Pasture Barn
50, 51 Sconset House and Barn
53 Sconset Barn
54, 55 Sconset Buildings
56, 57 Baxter Road
58, 59 Low Beach, Sconset

EPILOGUE

62, 63 Madaket Beach House
64 Great Point Lighthouse 1784/1986
65 Sankaty Lighthouse 1848
66, 67 Brant Point Lighthouse 1746
68, 69 Auld Lang Syne, Sconset 1675
70, 71 Richard Gardner III House, 1723, Town
73 The Old Mill 1746
74, 75 Old Spouter, Lower Orange Street
76, 77 The Oldest House 1686
78 Pacific Bank 1818
79 Unitarian Church 1809
80 Lifesaving Museum
81 Marsh
82 Upper Harbor, Wauwinet
83 Polpis Harbor
84 Sunset, Madaket
85 Sunset, Dionas

ACKNOWLEDGMENTS

To my wife Rachel for letting me work outside of the box.

To all those who have given me creative inspiration and
helped me to know and love Nantucket:

Walter Beinecke, Mimi Beman, Peter Brown, Dick Denby, Lynn Foster,
Cary Hazlegrove, David Lazarus, Tom Mleczko, Michael O'Mara,
Albert Ottison, Karl and Susan Ottison, Lucinda Young.

A special thanks for the help given by the Nantucket Conservation Foundation
and the Nantucket Historical Association.

I am grateful to past friends Bruce Killen and Stephen Swift
Lastly, to my Great, Great, Grandfather, Christopher Capen
and my mother, Julie Capen Lapham Dunlap.